CW00806434

The Rural Idyll

The Rural Idyll

Edited by
G. E. Mingay

Routledge

First published 1989
by Routledge
11 New Fetter Lane, London EC4P 4EE

Typeset in 10/12 Times Linotron 202
by Input Typesetting Ltd, London
Printed in Great Britain
by T. J. Press (Padstow), Cornwall

British Library Cataloguing in Publication Data

The rural idyll
1. England. Rural regions. Social life, history
I. Mingay, G. E. (Gordon Edmund)
942′.009′734

ISBN 0–415–03394–2

Contents

List of plates

The contributors

C. W. Chalklin, Reader in History, University of Reading

Jill Franklin, late Specialist in Victorian country houses

Michael Havinden, Senior Lecturer in Economic History, University of Exeter

Louis James, Professor of Victorian and Modern Literature, University of Kent at Canterbury

W. J. Keith, Professor of English, University College, University of Toronto

Philip Lowe, Lecturer in Countryside Planning, University College, University of London

G. E. Mingay, Emeritus Professor of Agrarian History, University of Kent at Canterbury

Alan Rogers, Senior Lecturer in Rural Planning, Wye College, University of London

Rosemary Treble, Historian of Victorian art

Editor's note

The essays which make up chapters 1–6 of this book first appeared *The Victorian Countryside* (ed. G. E. Mingay, London: Routledge & Kegan Paul, 1981) and are reprinted here by kind permission of the authors. Chapters 7, 8, and 9 were specially commissioned for this new volume.

Introduction

At the beginning of Victoria's reign the landowners of England held undisputed sway over the countryside. Their political, economic, and social hegemony was symbolized by their country houses, the overt expression of wealth, status, and significance. The house and its grounds varied in size, of course, according to the position and resources of the owner: a vast mansion standing isolated in a park of several square miles was the mark of the highest territorial eminence; a more modest establishment reflected a lesser place in landed society but still served to assert the relative affluence and superiority which gentry families enjoyed over the generality of ordinary country folk. Many of the houses were old, built long before, though perhaps added to and embellished over the centuries, expressing the association of ancient families with particular locations; others were new or entirely rebuilt, and not infrequently denoted the recent arrival into landed society of families freshly risen from a humdrum background of counting-houses, banking and shipping offices, or even factories. According to their resources they all, old and new, built solidly for durability, lavishly for prestige, and thoughtfully for comfort, as the late Jill Franklin explains in the chapter which opens this volume.

Country houses continued to be built, with fashionable variations in size and style as seemed appropriate, and increasingly they were built by newcomers, especially towards the end of the nineteenth century. With the costs of country-house life rising and the returns from land falling, the most recent arrivals in the countryside preferred, as Jill Franklin notes, more modest settings, and even ones which had no supporting estate, thus avoiding all trouble over tenants and rents. The problems of properties found now to be over-large, and their disposal as landed incomes declined in the later decades of the century, could as yet be solved only occasionally by sale to a wealthy businessman or conversion to some other use. The era of large-scale disposal of estates and houses was to arrive with the Great War and its aftermath.

Similar changes influenced the landowners' investment in model villages. Earlier in the nineteenth century the inspiration for such artificialities had sprung from the rise of Romanticism and the passion for the picturesque, as Michael Havinden recounts in his treatment of this topic. As time went by not only did the style of such villages change but landowners' interest in them declined. Cottage building, picturesque or otherwise, might produce aesthetic satisfaction and a rewarding sense of fulfilling one's social responsibilities: it did not, however, produce profits, rather the reverse. Increasingly it was the *nouveaux-riches*, the wealthier new proprietors who could draw on large resources of trade, industry, or commerce – philanthropists like Lord Wantage at Lockinge and Ardington – who were able to shoulder the burden of cottage building together with its ramifications of sports grounds, halls, reading rooms, and allotments. And gradually estate villages were supplemented by the planned and carefully controlled villages of industrialists, such as Street in Somerset, the development of C. and J. Clark, shoemakers; Port Sunlight, the creation of the Levers, soap manufacturers; and Bourneville and New Earswick, achievements of Cadbury and Rowntree, chocolate producers. Subsequent innovations in rural settlements were more and more likely to be the results of new irruptions of industrial growth in the countryside or the somewhat bleak excrescences of local housing authorities.

Villages, planned or not, could not exist in a vacuum. They needed farms or factories for employment, roads and railways for transport, and the various services offered by country towns. Such towns, found in every part of the countryside at a distance of ten or fifteen miles apart, furnished the commercial outlets of markets and fairs, a wider range of crafts and trades than even the larger villages could afford, and the services of professional men such as bankers, solicitors, estate agents, and doctors. Country towns varied in their size and activities according to location; some had cottage industries, workshops, and even small factories, while those on the coast also boasted some seaborne trade and fishing, and perhaps summer visitors.

But eventually, in the later decades of the nineteenth century, as C. W. Chalklin tells us, the impact of machine-made goods from outside weakened the position of country-town crafts. The sails of flour mills ceased to turn, malthouses decayed, small local breweries no longer flavoured the atmosphere, and home workers in traditional domestic trades put aside their tools and migrated to local factories or took up other occupations. Some country towns expanded, it is true, transformed perhaps into railway centres, or studded by the chimneys of large-scale works concerned with iron founding and engineering, textiles, hosiery or gloves, furniture making, paper, bricks, cement, and a wide variety of other products. The process of concentration made some towns into important regional centres but left others to shrink and decline, their markets and crafts abandoned or reduced in significance. Some of these towns fell into an unwonted somnolence, later to be revived perhaps by an influx of car- or train-borne commuters, by new kinds of trade, and the arrival of branches of modern twentieth-century industry.

The Victorian countryside of the painter was related in some degree to the picturesque romanticism of Gothic country houses, pseudo-medieval halls, and the thatched roofs and latticed windows of model villages. Their simple rustic scenes of cottage life, as Rosemary Treble remarks, were as unreal as the fantasies composed of stone, brick, and mortar. This nostalgic escapism, however, was to be countered by the social realists of a subsequent generation. Over-sensitive critics complained that their realism was indeed a shade too real for comfort, but most Victorian painters were not politically involved, and the landscapes and country scenes of the 1860s and 1870s sought rather to portray the untamed elemental countryside, 'to represent God's work in nature at its most unremitting' (Treble, p. 57). England failed to produce a Millet or a Courbet, but its landscape artists catered effectively for 'the profound nostalgia of the urban middle classes for their rural past' (Treble, p. 59).

Louis James remarks in his essay on nineteenth-century literature that the use of the landscape to reflect moral character goes back to the origins of the novel, and may be found, for instance, in Fielding and Jane Austen. The poets, such as Wordsworth, Robert Bloomfield, John Clare, William Barnes, and Tennyson, also searched to express the nature of country life in their various ways, resorting even to experiments with dialect. Social protest was another theme, taken up in particular by Clare and Barnes, and more positively by George Crabbe and Ebenezer Elliott. However, the realities of rural life came fully to the novel only with Hardy, who dealt with the unvarnished truth of a contemporary countryside rather than with a remote, idealized one. Hardy's social sensibilities, however, were accompanied by an appreciation of natural beauty and the seasons which was as profound as that of Wordsworth. In Hardy were combined 'a deep poetic sense of nature with an immediate understanding of the issues and evolution of history' (James, p. 74).

Social realities pervaded in varying degrees the work of those writers who observed rather than romanticized the countryside. Trollope's 'congenial portrayal' of landed society, as W. J. Keith puts it, was certainly at odds with the more earthy one of Hardy, and Trollope glossed over the injustices, the antagonisms, the poverty so bitterly attacked by William Cobbett. Cobbett's view of land was essentially a hard-headed one: what mattered was its capacity to produce, and how well or badly it supported its poorer inhabitants. Much of what failed to interest Cobbett – topics such as country sports, scientific farming, and gypsies – was described by a different breed of travelling author, William Howitt. And gypsies, together with such outlandish characters as prizefighters, horse-traders, tinkers, jockeys, and roadgirls, featured in George Borrow's nostalgic treatment of an older, more virile scene that was in course of disappearing, while Surtees brought a dash of satire to his humorous accounts of the adventures of a cockney master of foxhounds at large in the unaccustomed sphere of traditional hunting squires. In Richard Jefferies vivid reporting of the rural scene of the Great Depression years was combined with informative detail of country life and impressionistic pictures of rustic beauty. All was aimed at an urban audience, one which liked to read about the countryside but did not want to have its enjoyment spoiled by too strong an infusion of brutal reality. Much more matter of fact was Rider Haggard's *Rural England*, a detailed account of his discussions of current farming problems with landowners, agents, and farmers at the turn of the new century.

But in the end it is Hardy who provided a 'profound analysis as well as an unrivalled representation of nineteenth-century rural life and landscape' (Keith, p. 87). In general, it might be argued, Victorian literature as a whole offered a real, rather than ideal, picture of the contemporary life on the land. By the 1890s, the time of Hardy's last Wessex novels, the forces of change in the countryside had become very strong. The next twenty years were to see the recovery of farming after two decades of depression, a significant improvement in the position of the farmworker, and – most extraordinary to observers whose memories went back any distance – an irreversible decline in the territorial integrity of great estates and in the fortunes of those who owned them. These changes had to do with market forces, prices, profits and rents, and taxation. They had to do also with new concerns with the land itself.

As Alan Rogers notes in the first of his two discussions, the major interrelated themes in the changing land-use structure of the twentieth century were conservation and state intervention and planning. The second theme combines two different elements: a concern to regulate the farming industry so as to improve the efficiency of agricultural production and, as a result, to enhance the incomes of the producers; and the control of rural land use in order to protect it from 'excessive urban incursion and thereby to leave it to its "proper" custodians, the farmers'. As a consequence, despite all the pressures resulting from the spread of industry and new housing into former rural preserves, agriculture's share of the total land area of England and Wales fell by only a tenth between the years 1901 and 1981, while urban land, though rapidly increasing its share, still accounted in 1981 for well under an eighth of the total. And this in a period when the total population rose by over 50 per cent. But in the slow retreat of agricultural land there have been important changes in public conceptions of its uses, not least the much widened interest in the countryside for recreation and nature conservation. And in the process the lives of rural people became no longer remote or the subject of romantic idealism, but in many respects indistinguishable from the activities, attitudes, and interests of town dwellers.

In more recent years the countryside has been profoundly affected by a revival in the number of people residing there. The increase in commuters, daily carried to work by train and car, has wrought a transformation in the character of villages and their social structure. And accompanying this transformation are effects on the pattern of incomes, lifestyles, and housing, giving rise to strains and confrontations as the 'traditional' inhabitants find themselves outnumbered and outpriced by middle-class commuters and owners of second homes. The motor car has also opened the countryside to invasion by casual tourists, thus reducing the exclusiveness which for many of the resident newcomers is the essence of the 'rural idyll'. Nevertheless, as Alan Rogers concludes, it is possible to argue that there remains a distinctiveness in landscapes and lifestyles which is still highly attractive, and further, that the rural idyll will survive, perhaps in different forms, as 'the property of the masses'.

The newcomers to the countryside have been responsible in part for the growth of the conservation movement which Philip Lowe discusses in the final chapter. The roots of the movement, however, go back to the 1860s and grew as industrialism was increasingly seen as a threat to the environment. By the 1920s the pressures on the land were so ubiquitous as to require a more concerted defence, and rural preservation emerged as a significant force in British politics. The rescue of farming from stagnation in the inter-war doldrums was regarded as an essential prerequisite for checking urban encroachment and minimizing the flight from the land; though, ironically, it is the very economic success and technical progress of agriculture since the Second World War that has led to a changed perception of the role of farming. Now, the farmer, with his exemption from planning controls, his freedom to erect farm buildings however ugly and alien, to grub up hedgerows and pollute the atmosphere and water supplies with burnt straw and chemicals, has become the new threat to the survival of an attractive rural environment.

Meanwhile, open-air enthusiasts and naturalists demanded freer access to open country and the creation of nature reserves. The Second World War gave rise to shifts in government policy for rural preservation, as in so many spheres. Urban containment and green belts, national parks and nature reserves, and enhanced state support for farming, were major elements of the new ideology. One tangible result was a decline, by nearly a third, in the average annual loss of farmland to urban development. And an offshoot of the growth of ex-urban residents of villages has been the appearance of local conservation groups, concerned to oppose in detail those changes which might adversely affect their conception of what the countryside should be like. New conflicts between these (and their allies in national conservation organizations) and the farmers are bringing fresh tensions to the countryside of the 1980s.

The rural idyll is a changing concept: the countryside of the end of the twentieth century is very different from that of a hundred years ago, just as that was different from the countryside in previous eras. Each generation of country dwellers and observers sees what it wants to see in the land: romantic beauty, nostalgic traces of the rustic past, peace, tranquillity; despoiled landscapes, brutal intrusions of modernization, hurry, noise, pollution. The pressures of change and the forces of conservation will continue to struggle with each other for what they see as the 'right' kind of countryside for contemporary life. This book recounts the changing perceptions of the last century and a half, and in so doing may help us to understand more fully the issues and the forces that have influenced our view of the ideal countryside, past and present.

1

The Victorian country house

Jill Franklin

Victorian country houses are little known or visited, though well over a thousand are documented,[1] perhaps twice as many were built, and a very large number of them survive. They are extraordinarily varied in appearance, yet all of them make use to a greater or lesser extent of architectural elements borrowed from an earlier period, just as Georgian country houses had done. Fashion in historical style changed far more rapidly in the nineteenth century than it had done in the eighteenth, moving in sixty years from Italianate classical or Tudor and Jacobean to various kinds of Gothic, then on to English vernacular and finally round again to the classical English baroque. None of the new fashions completely ousted the previous ones, so that belated Italianate overlapped with the earliest neo-Georgian, while Elizabethan remained popular throughout the reign and after.

The great variety of styles in use at one time – and by no means all of them have been named – suggests that none was as universally satisfactory as Palladian had once been. Rapid social change had left country house owners as a class uncertain and divided over the image their houses should present, and in a single decade they could house themselves like feudal, Christian lords of the manor, classic squires, French renaissance monarchs, or yeoman farmers. Yet although period styles were sometimes copied so faithfully that it can be quite difficult to distinguish fifteenth- from nineteenth-century work, more often the total effect is as unmistakably Victorian as that of Rossetti's paintings after Dante or Tennyson's *Morte D'Arthur*.

The early Victorian house, whatever its style, normally had a rectangular main block two or three stories high, with a low even roof or identical Elizabethan gables, beneath which were regularly spaced rows of large sash windows. The elevations might be symmetrical or asymmetrical, but in any case were built up on a system of balancing horizontals and verticals, often with a single tower offsetting the low bulk of the house. Abberley

Hall (*c.* 1846) (plate 1) and Stoke Rochford Hall (1841–5) (plate 2) are in different styles, yet still have much in common. Ashlared stone was still the favourite building material, external colour was uniform, and decorative trim thin and rather meagre. With certain exceptions, such as Anthony Salvin's Peckforton Castle or Sir Charles Barry's Cliveden,[2] houses of this period have a slightly tentative air despite their size, as though their designers had lost momentum in the gap between the fading of classical ideals and the arrival of Gothic ones.

By the 1860s, more than half of all new country houses were being built in a Gothic style,[3] but it was different from the early Victorian variety for it was no longer chiefly surface decoration but had become to many architects the only possible means of expression. Yet Gothic architects faced the major difficulty in designing country houses that little medieval domestic architecture of any kind survived and even less could serve as a direct model, so that everything had to be adapted for modern use, and even then much had to be borrowed from ecclesiastical buildings. However, conviction prevailed over common sense, and neither architects nor owners saw anything incongruous in furnishing the hall with a portion of thirteenth-century nave arcade, as at the Hall in Scott's Hafodunos House, or in lighting the gentlemen's cloakroom with a lancet window, as was done at G. Somers Clarke's Milton Hall in Kent.[4] It was no odder, they might have said, than living behind the front of a classical temple.

The real force of Victorian Gothic came not from its church detail but from characteristics that it shared in varying degrees with other current styles. The most striking of these was a tremendous emphasis on height and a consequent narrowing and constriction of all proportions. It was accompanied by marked asymmetry and broken outline, as well as by what was called 'truth', which meant giving full expression on the outside to the function of the rooms inside. Consequently country houses were no longer four-square and spreading, but piled up and aspiring. Roofs became higher and more steeply pitched, the skyline more romantic than ever before in England. Fantastic spires and tourelles, wedges, pyramids, and hipped gables might be clustered together in one house over an equally varied façade, whose many kinds of windows were composed in asymmetric diagonals and triangles and in many different planes. The front door was no longer in the centre, and instead of windows matching left and right an oriel might be answered by a chimney breast or even by a blank wall; sometimes the base of the staircase window rose diagonally. 'Truth' also affected the attitude to materials. Stucco was a sham and rough-textured stone often thought preferable to ashlar because of the 'interesting variety' it could give.[5] Exposed brick was now seen as honest and might be handled with considerable virtuosity. Decoration had to be 'structural', that is, differently coloured, and sometimes aggressively contrasting building materials could be used to form stripes, diapers, and banded window heads. The Gothic country house looks tense and often restless; it lacks either classical magnificence or comfortable domesticity, but it has a powerful and dramatic quality all its own (plates 3, 4, and 5).

Gothic for country houses held first place for little more than twenty years. By the 1870s owners were beginning to want to incorporate a suggestion of comfort and cosiness. Norman Shaw, the greatest of Victorian country house architects, was the key figure in evolving out of Gothic a new style to answer this need.[6] It was called 'Old English'[7] and took its motifs from the cottages and farmhouses of the home counties, exploiting tile-hanging, half-timbering, casement windows with small leaded panes, and tall Tudor chimneys; or red brick might be set in friendly contrast to newly rediscovered white paint. All this variety would be assembled into a deceptively casual-looking asymmetry, as though the house had grown up at random over the years. Roofs were still broken up, windows were of all shapes and sizes but the ensemble was more informal, spread out, and welcoming than in Gothic (plates 6 and 7). It was also more bourgeois, so that those who chiefly wanted to look imposing still opted for stone-built Tudor.

Old English could be delightful, especially for houses that were not too big, but after a while there was a reaction in favour of a more unified, coherent look. It could be expressed in two ways. Some architects continued to use Tudor or vernacular motifs, though with less emphasis on correct period detail, building free and asymmetric compositions that were less cluttered and more abstract than those of the previous generation. Many of Edwin Lutyens's early country houses were designed in this so-called 'free' style (plate 8). However, clients who liked the style mostly wanted small to medium-sized houses: C. A. Voysey and Baillie Scott, who each developed a personal version of it, were never commissioned to design a really big house (plate 9). Where formality or grandeur was required, architects and their clients, feeling the need for strict symmetry and classical discipline, turned to the English baroque of Wren and the early eighteenth century. Norman Shaw's flamboyant Bryanston (plate 10) of 1889–94 and Chesters of 1890–4 were influential in setting country house fashion in this direction. Ernest Newton, Shaw's pupil, preferred a rather quieter Georgian or Queen Anne (plate 11), and Lutyens, too, added English classical to his repertoire. At the same time, Tudor and Jacobean houses became correctly symmetrical again (plate 12). So what with the various free styles, the ever-popular Tudor, and once again classical, the client of 1900 had as wide a choice for the style of his house as had his predecessor in 1837.

All Victorian country houses were planned in two virtually separate parts, the main or family block and the service wing. Each part occupied much the same ground area, but while the main block was designed to be conspicuous and elaborate, the service wing had to be 'invisible' like the servants themselves. For the sake of convenience the Victorians invariably put all the 'offices' on one side, where they might be screened off by bushes or banks of earth and were usually hidden from the principal garden. Complete concealment of the service wing was often impossible on the entrance front, in which case it was considered essential to be able to see instantly 'the one part of the edifice as superior and the other inferior'.[8] So the service wing was normally lower than the main block, often brick-built where the house was stone, and with all its detailing faithfully reflecting the social gradings within (plates 5, 10, and 12).[9]

Coming inside the early Victorian country house, the caller would find himself in a formal entrance hall, possibly top-lit and with a first-floor gallery giving access to the bedrooms. Several large and high reception rooms, all simply shaped, well lit and of classical proportions, would open off it on a clear and axially arranged plan. One of them would almost certainly be a billiard room, virtually a standard feature by the 1850s. Smoking in the main body of the house was still out of the question, and though a few early smoking rooms date from the later 1840s[10] they were well secluded, probably in the tower, for no taint of smoke must reach the principal rooms. The main innovation of the time, pioneered by Edward Blore, Anthony Salvin, and A. W. N. Pugin, was the revival of the medieval great hall, which was usually fitted up in Gothic, but could be Jacobean.[11] At first owners were a little uncertain how it should be used, so that in some houses it became the main hall, in others the dining room or a free-standing room kept for entertaining and various social functions.[12] Initially, it did not matter if the great hall had no very obvious function: at a time of social tension it evoked a comforting if unreal vision of feudal order, the lord and his docile peasantry carousing in harmony together (plates 13 and 14).

By the 1860s the country house interior had altered. The plan became non-axial and a great deal more complicated; routes were more confusing; corridors had more turnings and rooms now included a variety of oddly-shaped bays and were apt to be darker and gloomier than before. Whereas in the eighteenth and early nineteenth centuries saloons and suites might be included purely for display, each Victorian reception room was planned for a single precise function. The living areas for the different sexes and groups in the house were systematically sorted, and segregated accommodation was provided for each.

On the ground floor a masculine suite developed as a counterpart to the drawing room, which had always been feminine territory. Each sex might use the rooms in the other domain, but it was on sufferance rather than by right. The male suite developed round the library, which had been common ground in Regency days but gradually grew more masculine in furnishing and atmosphere, so that ladies seemed less in place there.[13]

Then the billiard room, which in the 1830s and 1840s was often linked to the drawing room, as at Osborne, came to be regularly placed next to the library, even though in some social circles ladies were always free to play (plate 15).[14] These two rooms, along with a gentlemen's cloakroom and a separate entrance, formed the nucleus of the suite, and the owner's study might also be included in it. By the late 1860s, when smoking in the main house had become more acceptable, the smoking room normally adjoined the billiard room. Finally, the gun room, a typical example of Victorian specialization, appeared about this time and often, though not invariably, formed part of the suite.

Between the gentlemen's rooms on one side and the ladies' rooms on the other, lay the neutral territory of the hall. At the beginning of the period it was still the little used, formal entrance; by the 1850s it had begun a remarkable transformation into the favourite family living room. Mentmore was one of the first houses whose hall was planned as a living room from the start.[15] By the 1870s many new country houses had an adaptation of a medieval great hall or classical saloon as their principal, most used reception room (plates 16–18). To us these halls feel too high and usually too public to make acceptable sitting rooms; to the Victorians they had the overriding advantage of being the only place in the house that was open plan and available at any time of day for use by members of either sex, by family or guests, dogs, even children.

According to Robert Kerr, author of a weighty book of 1864 on house planning, the Victorian gentleman's first requirement at home, which easily outweighed elegance, importance, or ornament, was 'quiet comfort for his family and guests'.[16] By 1900 it was easy for him to be very comfortable indeed, far more so than in 1837.

The most important single element in country house comfort was warmth, which was achieved by a mixture of traditional and new methods. English rooms had always been warmed by individual open fires and continued to be so throughout this period. Consequently every living room and every bedroom had its separate fireplace, whose grate had to be cleaned, its fire laid and lit daily, its coals carried and put on at frequent intervals. The Victorians loved their cheerful, glowing fires and saw no reason to economize either on fuel or labour; but even from their point of view the system had the great drawback of leaving the corridors and outlying corners unheated. The hall, too, was often difficult to keep warm: Mrs Charlton of Hesleyside, for instance, described her downstairs as 'a cavern of icy blasts'.[17]

This changed with the gradual introduction of central heating, starting with a few installations at the end of the eighteenth century. Hot air, hot water, and steam systems were all tried, but without any pumps to aid circulation it was necessary to rely on convection, so the pipes had to be two or three inches in diameter and the radiators or grilles of immense size. Controlling the boiler and maintaining an even temperature was extremely difficult and demanded considerable intelligence and skill. Central heating remained rare in the early nineteenth century, but despite the technical difficulties it was increasingly often included in new houses from the 1840s on, though at that time it was almost always confined to the hall and corridors. However, as more of the problems were solved principal rooms, too, were provided with radiators to supplement the fires, until by the end of the century heating could be taken for granted in a new house, though certainly not in an old one. The combination of central heating and open fires was, of course, hugely extravagant, but without doubt it was luxuriously comfortable too.

Heating problems were closely allied to those of ventilation. The Victorians were newly and fully aware of the importance of fresh air; they considered that breathing 'vitiated' air was dangerous to health, even to life, and one of their objections to full central heating was that it made the air unpleasant and stuffy.[18] But they were in a dilemma since they also hated draughts. So first they made doors and windows as tight fitting and draught proof as possible and reinforced them with screens and thick, heavy curtain materials, but then they had to reintroduce fresh air, not only for health but even more importantly to prevent the horrible discomfort of smoking chimneys: even the best-designed chimney will smoke if the only outside source of air is down the flue. So an enormous number of patent grates came on the market, designed to draw in air and consume smoke in a great variety of ways. None was ideally satisfactory. At the same time several systems of ventilation independent of the heating systems were invented. These often involved air ducts hidden in the walls or set in free-standing pipes; open grilles in cornice or ceiling, acting as outlets for vitiated air, were common.

Owners were probably wise to be cautious over central heating in its early days. They were less conservative about new forms of lighting. In 1837 country houses were still lit by a combination of candles and oil lamps, and many continued to be so. Gas light was already available, but it was far from satisfactory. Each country house had to manufacture its own gas in its own gas house and the resulting product was so dirty, hot, and smelly that it was unacceptable in the family rooms. However, it was considered good enough for the servants and was installed in service wings and corridors at least from the early 1840s.[19] Various experiments and improvements culminated in the invention of the gas mantle in 1886, by which time a high proportion of new houses had at least partial gas lighting; but by then it was really too late, for electric light had become practicable for domestic use in 1879 and was already being used in a few country houses by the 1880s.[20] Ten years later it was still far from reliable and extremely expensive to run, but when working it clearly outmatched all older forms of lighting in brilliance, cleanliness, and convenience.

Plumbing arrangements also improved markedly during this period. Every Victorian country house had its own, usually abundant, water supply, and this was piped right round the house, but at first with only a few outlets apart from the WCs and the housemaids' closets. The gentlemen's cloakroom probably had a basin with a cold tap, but there were no other plumbed-in washbasins anywhere. The bathroom was reserved for the master and mistress, with perhaps a second one for the nurseries. Guest bathrooms did not exist, and a guest washed with jug and basin and slop pail in the bedroom or dressing room, and bathed in a hip bath in front of the fire. Every drop of hot water had to be carried up the back stairs from the kitchen, and one manservant remembered carrying forty cans night and morning.[21] Piped hot water in the country house is not recorded in the architectural press until the later 1860s, and although there are probably instances of it being installed earlier it did not become standard even in new houses until the late 1870s or early 1880s.[22] Once piped hot water had arrived a few more bathrooms were usually, though not invariably, provided. Guests could now expect one to every two or three bedrooms, though only exceptionally one to every suite. Even the men and maidservants would have one apiece.[23] Plumbed-in washbasins never reached the bedrooms; it was felt that sleeping in a room with a plug hole connected to the drains was an unacceptable risk to health.

The Victorians had become very conscious of the connection between health and sanitation and gave much thought to the WCs which were provided in generous numbers. They nearly always had an outside window and usually a connecting lobby. Nor were the servants stinted, though as a precaution against smells in the house, they often had to make do with closets outside the main body of the house.[24] Drains and sewerage, too, received a great deal of attention. Glazed and impermeable drain pipes, pioneered by Henry Doulton, were obviously less hazardous to health, and there were advances, too, in the design of valves, traps, and devices for eliminating 'effluvia' or dangerous smells.[25]

Victorian country houses were built to last. They were intended as permanent family possessions and represented a long-term investment: part of the return was to be a conspicuous and powerful position in county society, in the future if not immediately. So they were constructed as solidly as possible; building methods were sound and careful, materials durable, nothing was shoddy or sham.

Costs varied enormously, naturally. As was only fitting, the Duke of Westminster spent the most: Waterhouse's remodelling of Eaton Hall cost over £600,000; but the Duke of Northumberland paid £250,000 for Salvin's remodelling of Alnwick Castle, Earl Manvers £170,000 for his new Thoresby Hall, also by Salvin, and Viscount Portman at least £200,000 and probably much more for Bryanston.[26] Several commoners' houses also cost huge sums. R. S. Holford's Westonbirt, built by Lewis Vulliamy, cost over £125,000, and John Walter's Bearwood by Robert Kerr over £120,000.[27] Lynford Hall by William Burn for Lyne Stephen, said to be the 'richest commoner in England', was reported, when up for sale in the 1890s, to have cost £145,000 to build, and the figure is by no means unlikely.[28] Others that must have cost as much or more include Waddesdon and Rhinefeld Lodge.[29]

At the other end of the scale it seems to have been impossible to build what the neighbours would have recognized as a country house for less than £6,000 or £7,000. A farmer in Hertfordshire became suddenly and unexpectedly richer when his land was found to yield coprolites or fossilized dung, used as a fertilizer. He decided to build a country house, Pirton Hall, for £5,000. 'I must beg to disabuse you of the notion of a *Mansion*', wrote his architect. For that price he would simply supply 'a good Country gentleman's house, plain and unpretending'. The final total was nearer £10,000, including stables, lodge, and kitchen gardens.[30] S. S. Teulon's Enbrook, near Hythe, which was only just large enough to be reckoned as a country house at that date (1853–5), cost about £7,300 for the house alone.[31]

With such a price range no single house can be taken as entirely typical, but David Brandon's Hemsted House in Kent (plate 6) can stand for many. The owner, Gathorne Hardy, later Earl of Cranbrook, bought the estate of just over 5,000 acres for £124,000 with money he inherited from his father's Staffordshire ironworks. The accepted tender for the house was £18,000, the final cost £23,000, but that sum did not include such items as the gasworks, grates, and furniture, which brought the complete bill to almost £33,000.[32]

Few really detailed sets of building accounts survive, but both at Westonbirt and Bearwood a little over half the building money went on wages, the balance on materials and transport. Wages ranged from £2 12s 6d. per week for the most highly skilled men to 10*s*. per week for labourers; but since the building process was hardly more mechanized than in the Middle Ages and very few items were prefabricated, huge numbers of men were needed on the site. Well over 400 men were employed at various times on Westonbirt, and 110 men sat down to the 'roofing supper' at Hemsted.[33] The size of the house was only one of the factors affecting the final price. Stone naturally cost more than brick, and stone itself varied in price according to quality; Chilmark was more expensive than Bath stone, for instance.[34] Bearwood, which was brick-built with lavish decorative trim in stone, can suggest relative costs. Some 4,250,000 bricks were made on the estate at a cost of £6,400 and the total bricklaying bill was just over £17,000. The stone, Mansfield for trim and York for paved floors, was just over £17,000, plus £850 for cartage, and the complete stonemasonry bill was over £26,000. Country houses needed huge amounts of timber, and at Bearwood the total figure for joinery work was over £40,000, nearly as much as the brick and stone together. Ironwork cost £9,000, including £4,000 on rolled iron joists, £4,600 went on plumbing and leadwork, £6,000 on the stoves and heating apparatus. Painting, glazing, and gilding came to only £7,000 together and plastering the same. The architect's commission was the standard 5 per cent of the cost of the house, plus travelling expenses.[35]

Most houses bear witness to the Victorian preference for durable materials. Many have no external paintwork at all: Mentmore had copper window frames, other houses had unpainted oak or teak. Indoors the servants' wing would have its walls plastered and painted, but in the reception rooms wood panelling or tooled leather hangings were often preferred (plates 14, 17, and 18). Consequently far less maintenance was necessary than in the days of stucco outside and lavish paintwork inside.

After an owner had decided how much to spend on building his new house, he next had to work out the maximum number of servants he could afford to keep. The plan of the house was geared to this figure. Of course servants were essential to domestic comfort, but above a certain size of household, say fifteen indoor servants, the precise number made little difference to the family's standard of living, though a considerable one to its status. Thus livery servants, who for much of the time were of little practical use, had a function merely in being conspicuously on view. Such an attitude to domestic service was possible and even made sense because throughout the nineteenth century domestic servants, women especially, were cheap and available in huge numbers; and of all the domestic jobs to be had those in the country house were among the most sought after.[36]

Consequently, although a great deal of thought was given to the smooth running of the house, good planning had absolutely no connection with labour saving, at least until towards the end of the period. Running hot water in the bathroom was a success not because it saved the servants carrying the cans but because it saved the guests having to wait for them. A well-planned house was one where the work could be reasonably shared out between a fixed number of servants, and so organized that they could each carry out their duties without getting in each other's way. To achieve this the Victorians classified the various jobs, providing a separate and appropriate place in which each was to be carried out. In earlier times the brushing of the family's clothes had been done in the servants' hall; a Victorian house had a separate brushing room.

One aim of the planning was to ensure that men and women servants had no unnecessary contact with each other, not only in the sleeping quarters but also in the course of their work: segregation would promote efficiency and propriety at one and the same time. It was equally important that the servants should not disturb the family's illusion of privacy, even though everyone knew they were there and that it was impossible to keep secrets from them.[37] Separate entrances, staircases, and corridors brought home who was who and prevented unnecessary contact. The architect of Rhinefeld Lodge noted that 'an important feature of the planning of this house is that no servant's room or office, with the exception of the attic dormers, can overlook the grounds at any point'.[38]

The work of the country house was organized, as in the eighteenth century, into three departments, headed by the cook, the butler or steward, and the housekeeper. These three, and personal servants such as the ladies' maids, were known as 'upper servants' and were sharply differentiated in duties and status from the under servants, who did the really hard and menial work. Demarcation lines were rigid and no servant, even the lowliest, could be asked to do the work of another.[39] Also, in any large house much of the servants' time was spent in waiting on each other. T. F. Buxton, the owner of Easneye, near Ware, had twenty-three servants and reckoned that fifteen waited on the family and eight on the fifteen.[40] It is no wonder that from 1830 to 1870 or later the service wing grew more elaborate and occupied more space in relation to the main house than ever before.

One early Victorian house can give an idea of the general principles of layout. Stoke Rochford Hall in Lincolnshire (plates 2 and 19) was built in 1841–5 at a cost of some £60,000 for Christopher Turnor, a hereditary landowner.[41] His architect was William Burn, famous for his skilful planning.[42] Each household department had its own cluster of rooms. The butler, who had five menservants under him in 1871, had his section in the basement under the main house.[43] This arrangement gave the footmen easy access to the hall and front door, though the basement bedrooms for the menservants were much disliked.[44] Next came the housekeeper's section, placed beneath the exclusively family part of the house, known as the 'private wing', so that the housekeeper had easy communication with her mistress in the boudoir overhead. The housekeeper's room was used as her office and sitting room, and often as a dining room by the upper servants. In 1871 the housekeeper had under her four housemaids, two still-room maids, and three laundry maids. Further on came the kitchen department, staffed by the cook, two kitchen-maids, a scullery maid, and a dairy-maid. It was arranged round a kitchen court, one side of which held the servants' hall, the only room where the under servants could legitimately spend any time in the company of the opposite sex. The laundry and the brew house were the furthest from the main house because of the smell and steam.

Perhaps the most remarkable feature of the plan to modern eyes is the distance from kitchen to dining room, some 40 metres. This was no lapse on the architect's part but rather an instance of good planning, since the Victorians were terrified of kitchen smells, cabbage water above all.[45] Far better for the footman to walk the length of two cricket pitches than risk tainting the dining room. Then each staircase has its meaning and function. Only guests and adult members of the family might use the principal staircase from the hall to the first floor; housemaids, footmen, and children were relegated to different and minor backstairs. A little later houses could have a staircase reserved for visiting bachelors, a nursery stair, a young ladies' stair.[46] All this multiplication made still more work. It was only towards the end of the century that planning sometimes became a little simpler: the kitchen could be a little closer to the dining room, the service wing contracted slightly, staircases were fewer. But where comfort was concerned labour saving meant nothing.

Before he reached the comforts of the house the visitor had to pass the lodge, whose style would warn him what to expect of the mansion, then drive through the park or grounds. Few of the landscaped parks surrounding the Victorian country house were entirely of Victorian creation. So much landscaping had been done in the eighteenth century that after 1840 comparatively few large new estates were assembled from untouched or agricultural land. Among the exceptions to this are Bylaugh Hall, Norfolk, a house of 1849–52, built in the middle of turnip fields and landscaped by W. A. Nesfield, the best-known landscape designer of the time; Waddesdon Manor, where the planting of well-grown trees created an instant park out of an outlying portion of the Stowe estate; and Cragside, where William Armstrong made a romantic Rhineland forest grow on a bare Northumberland hillside.[47] But Aldermaston Court, Tortworth Court, and Bearwood were more typical: each replaced an earlier house whose park had been landscaped in the eighteenth or early nineteenth century, leaving the Victorians to make only comparatively minor alterations.[48]

In any case, whether it was an entirely new creation or not, the Victorian park would have startled an eighteenth-century gentleman a good deal less than its mansion. It was likely to reflect the ideas and practice of Humphry Repton and the effect aimed at in the wider landscape was still one of heightened naturalness. The free outlines of the planting emphasized the contours of the slopes and opened up views to the distant horizon, suggesting or exaggerating the extent of the estate. If nature permitted, a river or stream was dammed to form a sinuous lake in the middle distance, its banks partly shaded by trees and shrubs.

The Victorians liked to use a great variety of species in their planting and were particularly fond of conifers and plants with dark shiny leaves, such as laurels and rhododendrons. Many new species from all round the world became available in the early Victorian period, including hollies, weeping trees, conifers, bamboos; monkey puzzles were in plentiful supply from 1843, Wellingtonias from 1853.[49] Their novelty of form or exotic colour were always eagerly welcomed, but plants were now juxtaposed with a botanist's eye rather than a painter's. J. C. Loudon thought Kent and Repton had 'indiscriminately mixed and crowded together' their bushes and trees, and that it was better to arrange them by species according 'to their kinds and forms' in the way that would 'best display the natural form and habit of each'. He called this the 'Gardenesque' style, and it led on to the fashion for specimen gardens and the planting of specimen trees (plate 20).[50] The Victorians also liked strong colour contrasts and a romantic overall effect. The eighteenth-century grounds of Stourhead were designed to be neat, trim, and idyllic. By the nineteenth the outlines were blurred, the planting was lusher and denser, and far more dark-leaved plants were used; the rhododendrons were Regency but the peak years for conifer planting were the early 1850s.[51]

The treatment of the approach altered too. The Victorian country house was not for public viewing, as the eighteenth-century one had been. Privacy was now much more important than grand initial display, and in order to keep the park and the garden front of the house secluded the Victorians made the carriage drive wind round the edge of the park, so that the visitor caught his first sight of the gardens, lake, and main prospect only after passing through the house. Many older houses, Hatfield among them, had their main entrance moved round to what had once been the back.

The immediate surroundings of the house altered much more than the outer park. Repton had often used terraces and flower gardens as a transition between the man-made bulk of the house and the apparently natural park, but now a formally planned, carefully detailed, small-scale foreground became one of the most characteristic, if impermanent, features of early and mid-Victorian grounds. Sir Charles Barry gave many of his houses a setting or intermediate zone of Italianate terraces bounded by stone balustrades at different levels, often linked by formal stairways and punctuated by urns and possibly statuary. He called it 'architectural gardening'[52] (plate 21). The terraces themselves were laid out with elaborate and symmetrically designed parterres, edged with box, and filled with coloured stones or tightly packed, highly coloured bedding plants. Beyond the parterres would be shrubberies, rose gardens, and specimen gardens, until finally the park proper was reached.

In the later part of the century bedding-out became rather less popular, and the parterres were often replaced by borders that were still formally and symmetrically laid out but were now planted with what were referred to as 'old-fashioned flowers', hardy if humble perennials, freely arranged as in a cottage herbaceous border.[53] William Robinson and Gertrude Jekyll were the principal propagandists for such planting, advocating softer and subtler colour schemes and stressing the importance of attractive foliage and good ground cover.[54] Architectural features such as pergolas, stone-bordered pools, and garden pavilions were often included, and as the zones were no longer so rigidly demarcated the flower garden took on some of the manufactured naturalness of the park. At the very end of the century another reaction brought a revival of formal and symmetrical gardening in keeping with the new symmetry in architecture.[55] Both kinds of garden design flourished until the First World War.

By 1900 there was little demand for landscaping on the grand scale. The number of houses built, like Hemsted, as the centre of a landed estate had reached its peak in the 1870s, and it dropped continuously from then on.[56] The agricultural depression and the competition of cheap foreign food had caused a considerable fall in rents and the sale value of land, especially in arable country. Many owners of large estates who were dependent on their rents had to cut expenditure; others were forced to try and sell out altogether. The result was something of a glut of country house estates on the market.[57] By the 1890s it was easy and far cheaper than formerly to buy or rent a period house. Such famous houses as Houghton Hall, Hesleyside, and Apthorpe were up for sale in the 1880s and remained on the market for years.[58] This naturally made it even harder to sell modern country houses. Octavius Coope, MP, the brewer, paid £120,000 for his estate in 1878 and spent £30,000 on building his house, Berechurch Hall. but when he put the estate up for sale ten years later the best offer (not accepted) was £80,000, and in 1894 he had still not disposed of it.[59] In these circumstances the idea of building a new country house inevitably lost much of its glamour.

At the beginning of the reign hereditary landowners had built three times as many houses as the *nouveaux riches*. By the 1880s they were building only half as many, and by the 1890s fewer than a fifth.[60] Those of them who could still commission large houses almost certainly had non-agricultural money, like Lord Portman, paying for Bryanston with his London rents. New men were still building very large country houses, though fewer than before, but towards the end of the century their money probably came from different sources too. They were now more likely to be in biscuits, general groceries, or soap, like G. W. Palmer of Huntley & Palmer and Marlstone House, Berkshire, Hudson Kearley (later Lord Devonport) of International Stores and Wittington House, Buckinghamshire, and his neighbour, Robert Hudson of Hudson's soap and Danesfield. South African gold paid for Cavenham Hall in Suffolk and for Tylney Hall in Hampshire. Shiplake Court was built by a stockbroker, Wightwick Manor for an ink and paint manufacturer. And, as before, bankers, shipowners, and brewers all built country houses.

It was nothing new for rich and successful members of the middle classes to move into the country, but now, instead of transforming themselves into landed gentry with country houses surrounded by estates of hundreds if not thousands of acres, they often preferred a medium-sized house with grounds of tens of acres, grounds which in all probability had originally belonged to some great landowner forced to sell off outlying parcels of land in order to keep going.

Professional men, as well as business men of all kinds, now commissioned these houses in the country. Much of Norman Shaw's work in the home counties was for successful Royal Academicians, Philip Webb's last house, Standen, was for a solicitor, Leonard Stokes's Thirteover for a barrister, and Voysey's Greyfriars for the writer, Julian Sturgis. Although Shaw and Lord Portman ensured that no one could make a mistake about Bryanston, the look and style of a house in the country such as Redcourt (plate 11) was often indistinguishable from that of a newly built, modest country house with a proper estate. True, the grounds were small and the owner could not hope to move in county society, but still his house was a well-built and valuable piece of property and he could live in it in the greatest comfort without having to worry about tenants and rents. No wonder that by 1900 many owners preferred the appearance of a country house to the reality.

Notes

1 Principally in the architectural journals: *Civil Engineer and Architects' Journal*, 1837–67; *Builder*, 1843– ; *Building News*, 1855– ; *Architect*, 1869– ; *British Architect*, 1874– ; *Academy Architecture*, 1889– ; *Studio*, 1893– ; *Builders' Journal*, 1895– ; *Architectural Review*, 1896– ; *Country Life*, 1897– ; and in Pevsner, 1951–74.

2 Peckforton Castle: British Architectural Library, drawings coll., W8/12 (1–15); *Country Life*, 1965, CXXXVIII, 284–7, 336–9; Girouard, 1971, 73–7. Cliveden: *Builder*, 1850, VIII, 318; Barry, 1867, 119–22.

3 Franklin, 1973, 15, 19.

4 *Building News*, 1874, XXVII, 254.

5 *Civil Engineer*, 1860, XXIII, 129.

6 Girouard, 1971, 44–9, 141–6, 158–60; Saint, 1976, 24–53.

7 Eastlake, 1872, 110, 131, 135, 339.

8 Kerr, 1864, 226.

9 Scott, 1857, 157; Stevenson, 1880, II, 142; *Civil Engineer*, 1864, XXVII, 181.

10 Osborne House, 1845: Girouard, 1971, 25; Abberley Hall, *c*. 1846: sale catalgoue, BM Maps, 137b, 11 (16); Bricklehampton Hall, 1848: sale catalogue, BM Maps 137b 11 (17); Mentmore Towers, 1850–5: *Builder*, 1857, XV, 738–40.

11 Blore: Goodrich Court, 1828–41, V & A Drawings 87430, 1–40; Nash, 1845, 12. Moreton Hall, 1841–3, BM Add. *mss* 42027, vol. 28, 15–17. Salvin: Harlaxton Manor, 1828–38, *Country Life*, 1906, XX, 522–32; 1957, CXXI, 704–7; Hussey, 1958, 239–48; Pevsner, *Lincolnshire*, 1964, 561–5; Pugin: Scarisbrick Hall, 1837–45, Pevsner, *North Lancashire*, 1961, 218–23; Stanton, 1971, 28–33; Girouard, 1971, 60–4. Bilton Grange, 1841–6, Stanton, 1971, 176, 200.

12 Dining room at Great Moreton Hall and Bilton Grange, free-standing at Bayons Manor and Hall, Barnstaple (see Pevsner, *North Devon*, 1952, 92).

13 Loudon, 1833, 796; Gore, 1849, I, 288; Kerr, 1864, 129; cf. Eliot, 1876, bk 5, ch. 6.

14 Fullerton, 1847, I, 9; Ticknor, 1864, 358; Yonge, 1853, 35; Cavendish, 1927, I, 145; Knightley, 1915, 226.
15 Disraeli, 1938, 159; *Builder*, 1857, XV, 738–40.
16 Kerr, 1864, 73.
17 Charlton, 1949, 176.
18 *Builder*, 1854, XII, 288; Stevenson, 1880, II, 221.
19 For instance at Worsley Hall, Lancashire: British Architectural Library, drawings coll., Worsley Account Book, 12–23 October 1843.
20 Girouard, 1971, 17.
21 Lanceley, 1925, 177.
22 Didsbury Towers, 1865: *Builder*, 1873, XXXI, 222, 722. Crown Point, Norwich, 1865: 1872 sale catalogue, Norwich Public Library. Bayham Abbey, 1869–72: *Builder*, 1871, XXIX, 985–7. Wykehurst Park, 1871–4: *Builder*, 1872, XXX, 565–7; Murphy, 1883, 90.
23 Stevenson, 1880, II, 75; Muthesius, II, 56.
24 For instance at Clouds, plans British Architectural Library, drawings coll., V14 (11–216). Cf. Westonbirt, British Architectural Library, drawings coll., R. S. Holford, letter 16 November 1865.
25 Stevenson, 1880, II, 265–74; Saint, 1976, 180–4.
26 Eaton: Smith, 1971, II, 387–99. Alnwick: Pevsner, *Northumberland*, 1957, 69. Thoresby: Thoresby Account Book, Nottingham University Library. Bryanston: Saint, 1976, 432.
27 Bearwood: Berks. RO: Walter Papers, Building Accounts, 1864–70. Westonbirt: Westonbirt Papers and Fortnightly Returns, 1864–71, British Architectural Library, drawings coll.
28 *Estates Gazette*, 31 December 1898.
29 Waddesdon: Fowler, 1894, 171–2. Rhinefeld: *Builder*, 1889, LV, 121–2.
30 Herts. RO: Pirton Papers, 71830–72035; Hanscomb, 1967, 159.
31 *Builder*, 1854, XII, 486–7.
32 *Builder*, 1862, XX, 242–3, 259; first Earl of Cranbrook, *Private Diaries*, and Hemsted Account Book, East Suffolk RO: HA 43/T501/286–306 and 178.
33 Westonbirt computed from Fortnightly Returns, see note 27; Hemsted: Cranbrook *Diaries*, 28 October 1860, see note 32.
34 Estimates and correspondence for Pangbourne Tower owned by Mr J. V. Hamilton.
35 Kerr, 1864, 223; *Builder*, 1884, LXVIII, 549; Thompson, 1963, 187.
36 Franklin, 1975, 221.
37 Disraeli, 1845, 157; Trollope, 1869, II, ch. 51; Kerr, 1864, 75; Lethaby, 1935, 99.
38 *Builder*, 1889, LV, 122.
39 Dana, 1921, 40.
40 Information from his grandson, Mr J. Buxton.
41 Pevsner, *Lincolnshire*, 1964, 644.
42 Kerr, 1864, 476; *RIBA Transactions*, 1869–70, series 1, XX, 121–4.
43 1871 census, PRO: RG 10/3357. (In the 1851 census, the jobs of the menservants are not given, and in 1861 the family and many of the servants were away.)
44 Horne, 1930, 236.
45 *Builder*, 1886, L, 87; Cholmondeley, 1897, 52.
46 Early bachelor stairs at Bearwood: Kerr, 1864, 3rd edn, 1871, plates 35, 36. Westonbirt: British Architectural Library, drawings coll., V7/3 (1–17).

Nursery stair at Highclere Castle (Sir Charles Barry): plans at house; young ladies' stair, Bearwood.

47 Bylaugh Hall: *Builder*, 1852, X, 517–19; *Building News*, 1869, XVI, 272ff. Waddesdon Manor: Fowler, 1894, 171–2; *Gazette des Beaux Arts*, 1959, series 6, LIV, 13–16. Cragside: Girouard, 1971, 143–4, 293–9; *Country Life*, 1969, CXLVI, 1640–3.

48 Aldermaston Court: *Country Life*, 1899, VI, 240–2; 1907, XXII, 54–9. Tortworth Court: *Country Life*, 1899, V, 592–6. Bearwood: *Country Life*, 1969, CXLIV, 964–7.

49 Hadfield, 1960, 314, 322–3.

50 Loudon, 1840, VIII.

51 Woodbridge, 1971, 14–18, 28–30.

52 Barry, 1867, 113–19.

53 Girouard, 1977, 152–8.

54 Jekyll, 1899; 1900; Jekyll and Weaver, 1912; Robinson, 1883; Clifford, 1962, 206–11.

55 Blomfield and Thomas, 1892.

56 Girouard, 1971, 6.

57 *Estates Gazette*, 8 January 1881, 14 October 1882, 14 July 1883, 6 February 1892, 4 January 1896.

58 *Estates Gazette*, 31 October 1885, 15 October 1887, 7 January 1888, 7 January 1893.

59 *Estates Gazette*, 7 January 1888, 6 January 1894.

60 Girouard, 1971, 6.

1 Abberley Hall, Worcestershire: an Italianate house by Samuel Daukes, built *c.* 1846 with an asymmetrically placed tower (from a sale catalogue, BM maps 137b, 11 (16)).

2 Stoke Rochford Hall, Lincolnshire, built 1841–5 by William Burn in typically early Victorian Elizabethan (National Monument Record. By kind permission

3 Bestwood Lodge near Nottingham by S. S. Teulon, 1862: asymmetry, broken outline, much structural decoration. The ‘chapel’ on the left was the servants’ hall (*Builder*, 1863, XXI, 639).

4 Possingworth Manor, East Sussex, by M. D. Wyatt, 1865–70: high Victorian verticality at its most extreme (*Builder*, 1868, XXVI, 713)

5 Hemsted House, Kent, by David Brandon, 1859–62: Jacobean asymmetry plus a high French roof over the tower and a diagonal staircase window. Now Benenden School and considerably altered (*Builder*, 1862, XX, 243).

6 Merrist Wood, Worplesden, Surrey, by Norman Shaw, 1875–7: stone, half-timbering, brick, and tile-hanging, brilliantly combined (National Monument

7 Lewins, Crockham Hill, Kent, by J. M. Brydon, 1876–83: the same ingredients as at Merrist Wood, used on a larger and taller house (*Building News*, 1883, XLIV, 750).

8 Avon Tyrell, Hampshire, by W. R. Lethaby, 1891–2: a late Victorian, free adaptation of Tudor (*Country Life*).

9 Perrycroft, Colwall, Herefordshire, by C. F. A. Voysey, 1893–4. The slate roof, roughcast walls, and strange chimneys are right outside the country house tradition (*British Architect*, 1895, XLIV, 437).

10 Bryanston, Dorset, by Norman Shaw, 1889–94: English baroque revived for the last Whig palace.

11 Redcourt, Haslemere, Surrey, by Ernest Newton, 1893–4: the beginning of Edwardian neo-Georgian, still with gables and some arts and crafts detail (National Monument Record. By kind permission of the Royal Commission on Historical Monuments of England).

12 Batsford Park, Gloucestershire, by Ernest George and Peto, 1887–93: a correct Tudor design showing the late Victorian return to horizontality and almost complete symmetry (National Monument Record. By kind permission of the Royal Commission on Historical Monuments of England)

13 An early Victorian version of a celebration in the medieval great hall of Haddon Hall (Jospeh Nash, 1838, new edn 1869, *The Mansions of England in the Olden Time*, plate XXV).

14 The dining hall at Bilton Grange, Warwickshire by A. W. N. Pugin, 1841–6: an early Victorian great hall with open timber roof (*Illustrated London News*, 1855, XXVI, 93. By kind permission of the Illustrated London News Picture Library).

15 The billiard room at Thurland Castle, Lancashire, by Paley & Austin, 1879–95, fitted out in a very masculine style with leather chairs and stuffed shooting trophies (National Monument Record. A Bedford Lemere photograph. By kind permission of the Royal Commission on Historical Monuments of England).

16 A classical, top-lit saloon at Dobroyd Castle, West Yorkshire, by John Gibson, 1865–9. Carpeted and with seats, this hall is still not really a living room. The upper galleries give access to the bedrooms (*Builder*, 1875, XXXIII, 953).

17 Rhinefeld Lodge, Hampshire, by Romaine Walker, 1888–90: a great hall in late Tudor style with hammerbeam roof. It includes a screens passage and minstrels gallery, but the small oriel window on the left opens out of the boudoir, where chaperones could sit comfortably and keep an eye on the party below (National Monument Record. A Bedford Lemere photograph. By kind permission of the Royal Commission on Historical Monuments of England).

18 Entrance hall, Thurland Castle, Lancashire: a single-storey hall used as a sitting room (National Monument Record. A Bedford Lemere photograph. By kind permission of the Royal Commission on Historical Monuments of England).

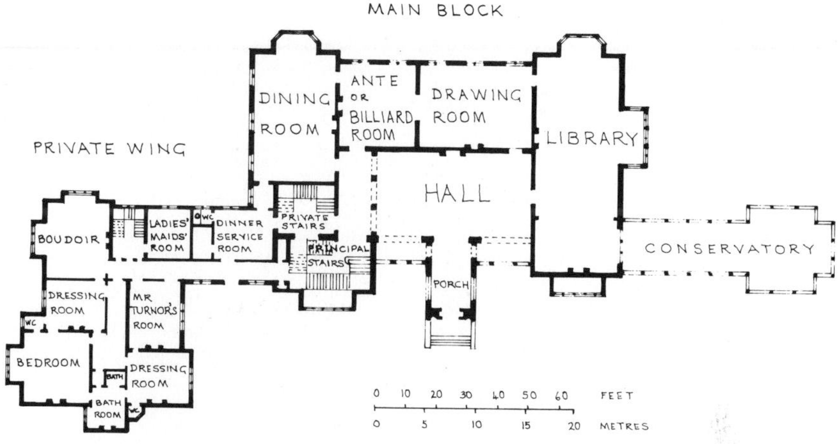

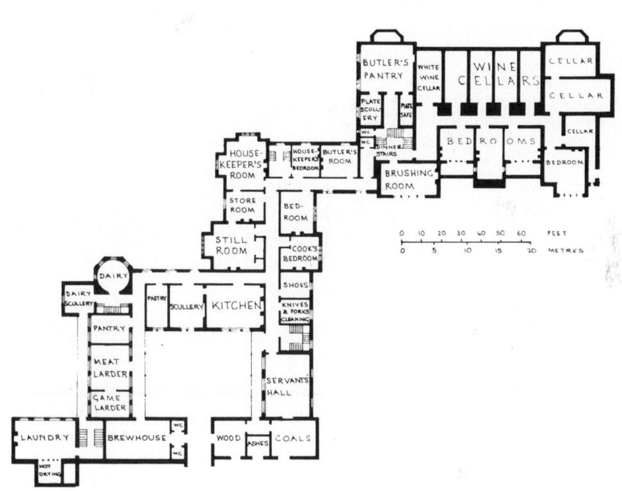

19 Plans of the principal floor and basement of Stoke Rochford Hall (redrawn from plans in RIBA drawings J12 (1–2), British Architectural Library, Drawings Collection).

20 A Victorian fernery: one kind of specimen garden (Alfred Smee, *My Garden, its Plan and Culture*, 1872, plate 10).

21 Architectural gardening by Sir Charles Barry at Shrubland Park, Suffolk, 1848 (Alfred Barry, *The Life and Works of Sir Charles Barry*, 1867, plate 17).

2

The model village

Michael Havinden

In discussing model villages it is as well to be clear at the outset what we are talking about since the term can be used to describe a wide variety of settlements. Probably the most generally recognized would be a planned village, such as Nuneham Courtney in Oxfordshire or Milton Abbas in Dorset. These were completely new villages, established on fresh sites because a landowner wished to remove an older village which had become an unsightly impediment to the development of his garden or park. These might perhaps be regarded as the ideal types, but they are not typical model villages. The typical model village would be more like East Lockinge in Berkshire (now Oxfordshire), which was an ancient historic village dating back to Saxon times; but which was partly resited and subjected to large-scale redevelopment, modernization, and 'prettification' by its owners, Lord and Lady Wantage, in the mid-nineteenth century.[1] The motives were partly aesthetic, partly philanthropic, and also practical – the belief that a well-housed and contented labour force would be more stable and more efficient than a miserable and discontented one.

However, although the typical Victorian model village was probably the handiwork of a paternalistic landlord, there were also other important types. These included co-operative settlement schemes inspired by people like Robert Owen and even Tolstoy; and the settlements established (albeit briefly) by the Chartists around the mid-century. There was also another type of growing importance: the model industrial village (of which Owen's New Lanark was perhaps the archetype) later developed in the direction of garden suburbs, such as Bourneville, near Birmingham; New Earswick, near York; and Port Sunlight, near Birkenhead. The term 'industrial' may also be understood quite broadly; it comprised villages devoted to mining and railways and also newly established small ports. Finally there were the seaside resort villages, of which Thorpeness in Suffolk was a representative type.[2]

If there was such a wide variety of model villages it is not surprising that the motivations and inspirations behind them should also have been many and varied. Before looking at these in more detail the chronological question should be briefly disposed of. Strictly speaking, a Victorian model village should be one built between 1837 and 1901; but these dates have no significance for the subject. The inspiration for builders often lay in changes of taste which occurred in the late eighteenth century (especially the rise of romanticism and the passion for the picturesque); whereas motivations like the desire to improve living standards, which were powerful in the late nineteenth century, continued on beyond 1901 without any break. So for purposes of convenience we shall take the century of peace between 1815 and 1914 as our time period. Although it was a period which witnessed more rapid and more profound changes than at any preceding time in British history, it was at least unified by one important influence which did not greatly change: namely the economic, political, and social ascendency of large (and frequently titled) landlords throughout the countryside.[3]

As we have seen, eighteenth-century model villages like Nuneham Courtney, Milton Abbas, and New Houghton, Norfolk, were really by-products of the landscaping activities of people like 'Capability' Brown and Nathaniel Kent. They excited no particular interest in themselves, and no powerful social, humanitarian, or aesthetic interests were involved in their construction. But by the nineteenth century this attitude was beginning to change. The villages were becoming objects of interest in themselves, although the aesthetic pleasure they were intended to give their owners was still a very much more powerful motive than any desire to improve the comfort or the well-being of their inhabitants: that was to come later.

It was the rise of the 'picturesque' movement in aesthetic fashion, and particularly the new interest in cottages as a specially important symbol, which seems to have been the initial inspiration for the early nineteenth-century model village. Many artistic trends, like the poetry of Byron and Wordsworth, and the landscapes of Constable, no doubt contributed to the generalized development of the mood, but it seems to have been the specific influence of two theorists which gave the movement its real driving force. These were William Gilpin and Sir Uvedale Price, Gilpin made tours in the latter part of the eighteenth century to encourage people to visit romantic and remote areas, such as Wales or north Devon, where wild and picturesque elements of an older age still survived. The enthusiasm of Wordsworth and Coleridge for Lynmouth Gorge, and later the Lake District, were part of this development. Gilpin was bored by the classical regularity of a village like Nuneham Courtney, which, although he admitted its superior convenience, seemed to him to lack the charm of the picturesque village. This charm was essentially based on a variety of styles in cottage building.

> When all these little habitations happen to unite harmoniously and to be connected with the proper appendages of a village – the winding road, a number of spreading trees, a rivulet and a bridge and a spire to bring the whole to an apex – the village is compleat.[4]

Sir Uvedale Price elaborated these sentiments in his *Essay on the Picturesque* (1794) where he encouraged landlords to remodel their estate villages along these lines, saying,

> there is, indeed, no scene where such a variety of forms and embellishments may be introduced at so small an expense, and without anything fantastic or unnatural, as that of a village; none where the lover of painting, and the lover of humanity, may find so many sources of amusement and interest.

Price's vision of the ideal village is well illustrated by his later comments on some cottages painted by van Ostade:

> Their outline against the sky is generally composed of forms of unequal heights, thrown into many different degrees of perspective; the sides are varied by projecting windows and doors . . . [and they demonstrate] what still may be shown in the playful variety and intricacy of buildings and their appendages, where space, elegance and grandeur are unthought of.[5]

It was not long before this alluring seed bore fruit, and strangely it was one of the masters of classical architecture, no less a person than John Nash himself, who designed the prototype for all later picturesque villages – Blaise Hamlet. The site was a few miles to the north-west of Bristol in the parish of Henbury, outside Blaise Castle, the mansion and park of the patron, the wealthy Bristol Quaker banker, J. S. Harford. Fortunately the nine ornate cottages built by Nash round a green in 1810–11 now belong to the National Trust, which has saved them from becoming totally engulfed in the surrounding suburbs of Bristol. Each cottage was built to a separate design and every device of the picturesque was employed to maximum effect – steeply pitched thatched roofs, dormer windows, rustic porches, and luxuriant creepers abounded; but Nash's greatest pride was in the lofty and elaborately ornate brick chimneys. Yet although Harford prided himself on his humanitarian interests (and campaigned against the slave trade) the accommodation offered in these cottages was extremely meagre. Admittedly they were intended for elderly people, but one small, dark living room downstairs and a couple of bedrooms in the eaves were all they provided – plus exterior washhouses and privies tucked away at the back. Clearly, aesthetic interests had triumphed over the residents' convenience, and this unfortunate example remained powerful throughout the nineteenth century.[6]

However, its influence declined from the 1840s when awareness of the appallingly bad housing conditions prevailing in so many rural areas became more widespread, and the desire to improve standards began to prevail over purely aesthetic considerations – although it was still hoped to combine the two. A leader in the movement for better standards of convenience and hygiene in cottages was Prince Albert, who became the active patron of the Society for Improving the Condition of the Labouring Classes, established in 1848. The society circulated plans for model cottages and, using the Prince Consort's example of improvements on the Crown estates, inspired landowners to rebuild cottages and remodel villages. The prince was responsible for improved cottages at Windsor and for model villages at West Newton (Sandringham estate, Norfolk) and Whippingham (Osborne estate, Isle of Wight). Soon some of the wealthiest landowners, like the dukes of Bedford, Devonshire, and Northumberland, were following the prince's example and setting a fashion which others were eager to emulate.[7]

There were, however, a number of problems which could easily deter all but the very wealthiest enthusiasts. The first was economic: cottages were a bad investment. Some figures from the Duke of Bedford's estates in the 1890s, relating to fifty-two cottages, show that the average cost of construction was £296. It was generally believed at the time that the gross rent should be about 10 per cent of the capital to cover rates, repairs, and incidentals, and allow some measure of profit on the investment. This would imply a yearly rent of £29.60. In fact the duke drew between £2.60 and £5.20 a year from these cottages, depending on their size. If we regard £4 a year as an average rent, the return on the investment was only about 1.3 per cent.[8]

This economic problem was compounded by the fact that the inhabitants of model cottages, or model villages, were frequently not the employees of landlords but of tenant farmers. Hence the landlord had no direct interest in subsidizing their wages. Where the model village was built primarily for domestic servants or estate employees, as at Edensor on the Duke of Devonshire's Chatsworth estate, this problem was minimized; but it must generally have acted as a deterrent. Another linked factor was the fear of erecting cottages whose occupants might become unemployed and hence fall on the poor rates. Indeed, so great was this fear that many landlords were more concerned with pulling down cottages than with erecting them. Villages of this type were known as 'close' villages, and a vigorous controversy raged on their relative merits and demerits as compared with 'open' villages, which became correspondingly overcrowded and insanitary.[9] In fact, in view of the strength and pervasiveness of the deterring factors, it is surprising that so many model villages were built.

The desire to retreat to a self-sufficient, co-operative rural settlement is very ancient. No doubt it embodies a faint folk memory of ancient village communities, as well as a reaction against the pressures and tensions of city life (which were reinforced in the nineteenth century by the dirt, disease, noise, and squalor of so many new industrial towns). Robert Owen was an early enthusiast, though most of his attempts to found rural settlements, both in England and America, were disastrous failures. One of his dissident disciples, William Allen, had better fortune though with Lindfield in Sussex, founded in 1831, and successfully based on small-holdings.[10] Fergus O'Connor tried to lead the Chartists in the same direction in 1848 after the failure of their mammoth petitions demanding the suffrage; but the few settlements which were established, like Charterville in Oxfordshire, Great Dodford in Worcestershire, and Snigs End in Gloucestershire, soon failed as social experiments, though they struggled on as centres for a few smallholders.[11]

Finally, there were the quite different motivations which inspired the builders of industrial villages. Their problem was usually to provide accommodation for a work-force which had to be attracted to a new site convenient for the mill – whether it was water or steam. Some of the early industrial villages like Turton and Egerton, Lancashire, which were built by the Ashworths for their employees, were relatively utilitarian,[12] but if the manufacturer was very successful, elements both of philanthropy and the desire to make a mark entered his motivation, as can be seen with Sir Titus Salt's Saltaire (1850s) near Bradford,[13] and Lord Leverhulme's Port Sunlight (1890s) near Birkenhead.[14]

As we have seen, the 'picturesque' style reigned almost unchallenged in the early nineteenth century, and only gave way slowly, and in scattered places, to rival styles. Some notable picturesque villages after Blaise Hamlet were Somerleyton in Suffolk, Ilam in Staffordshire, and Old Warden in Bedfordshire. Somerleyton, near Aldburgh in east Suffolk, was built for the great railway contractor, Sir Morton Peto, and was largely designed by the architect, John Thomas, in the 1850s. It is described by Gillian Darley as perhaps the most successful functioning picturesque village today.[15] Another good example is Ilam, set magnificently on a site in the Pennine dale country of north Staffordshire. It was designed by George Gilbert Scott in 1854 for a wealthy manufacturer, Jesse Watts Russell. Its garishly coloured tile-hanging is quite out of character with the vernacular architecture of the area, but gives the village an unmistakably 'picturesque' stamp.[16] Old Warden, Bedfordshire, built for the Ongley family around the middle of the century is another example well worth a visit, with much pretty thatch and elegant decorations.

One of the first rivals of the picturesque was eclecticism, which by its very nature can hardly be regarded as a style, and has, inevitably, produced some of the most extraordinary and eccentric of all the model villages. The picturesque style emphasized variety, but variety within the confines of a certain unity of approach and treatment. Eclecticism took this variety to its logical conclusion and removed all restraints. The best example is probably to be seen at Edensor, by Chatsworth, where the Duke of Devonshire built a remarkable collection of cottages in contrasting styles for his estate employees. The cottages are mostly detached and are well built of local stone, but their styles range from mock-Tudor, castellated Gothic, and Italianate renaissance to sturdy Swiss 'chalets', with a weird variety of intermediate decoration attached. In some ways it is the ultimate in model village architecture.[17] Although the picturesque and the eclectic were perhaps the most characteristic architectural manifestations of model villages, they did have some more sober rivals. An unadorned utilitarianism inspired Henry Roberts's cottage designs for the Society for Improving the Condition of the Labouring Classes, and it had a widespread influence, notably in villages on the Duke of Bedford's estate, and also those of the Duke of Grafton, like Potterspury in Northamptonshire.[18] The revived classic and Gothic styles had only limited influence, being too imposing for cottages; though elements of the former may be seen at Saltaire, and of the latter at Akroyden, near Halifax. These styles were not only too imposing but also too expensive.[19]

A more sensible response to the question of style was employed by those architects who sought to conform to the local vernacular style prevailing in the district while adding any minor improvements which may have seemed necessary. Thus at Penshurst in Kent the nineteenth-century additions conform more or less to the prevailing timber-framed Tudor style; and this approach was also adopted by Lord Wantage at East Lockinge, although admittedly some picturesque additions (particularly in the strange shape of dormer windows) were allowed to creep in.[20] This modified vernacular approach was fairly widespread. At Baldersby St James in Yorkshire William Butterfield adapted a local vernacular style in brick which was neo-Georgian except for its steeply pitched roofs. An even more modern type of vernacular was used by Raymond Unwin and Barry Parker at New Earswick, built for the Rowntree chocolate workers outside York, *c*. 1901–10. Here steeply pitched tiled roofs were combined with simple, often whitewashed, exteriors and fairly large windows, which were characteristic of what was then regarded as 'modern' architecture. As a garden suburb New Earswick, of course, occupies an intermediate position between village and town. Its ambience and feel are rural, but it is in fact part of the urban area of the city of York.[21]

Standards of housing varied very much from village to village, but with a tendency towards improvement as the nineteenth century progressed. The earliest picturesque villages, like Blaise Hamlet, provided only rather limited, dark and poky living space, but after the middle of the century most cottages offered a living room and kitchen downstairs, and three bedrooms above. The moral aspects of overcrowding particularly alarmed the Victorians, and it became increasingly seen as important that children should not share their parents' bedroom and that separate bedrooms should be provided for boys and girls. As families tended to be large this could still mean that three or four boys or girls might share a bedroom, but it was a great advance on the conditions which had often existed in the early part of the century.

An example of earlier conditions is provided by Ardington and Lockinge in 1860, before Lady Wantage and her husband started their work of amelioration. In later life (1907) she pungently described the old-world cottages as 'fast-decaying hovels through whose wattle and dab walls a walking stick could easily be thrust'.[22] When it was decided to remove part of the village which was too close to the Wantage residence to a more congenial site, Lady Wantage described the part to be destroyed as 'farm sheds, muck yards and hovels'.[23] The Wantages set about building the new model cottages with enthusiasm; and it may not be a coincidence that Lord Wantage had previously served as an equerry to the Prince of Wales, a position for which he had been selected by Prince Albert, some of whose enthusiasm for model cottages may have rubbed off on the young equerry. Lady Wantage stated:

> An architect was rarely employed; plans of buildings have always been made and executed under Lord and Lady Wantage's own superintendence. The picturesque character of the old style of cottage building, with its 'wattle and dab' walls, rough timber beams and thatched roofs, has been as far as possible retained, with the view of preserving the irregular character and charm of the old Berkshire villages.[24]

By the standards of the time these were sturdy and roomy cottages. Downstairs they had a living room 15 feet square and 8 feet 6 inches high, a small kitchen and outhouses containing a coalstove, a built-in copper with fireplace beneath for boiling water for washing, and an earth closet. Upstairs they had three bedrooms, one measuring 15 feet by 12 feet, and the other two 12 feet by 8 feet.[25] However there was one aspect of residence which never occurred to the Wantages: present-day residents have great difficulty getting any furniture into the upstairs rooms because of the steep roof gables and narrow twisting stairs.

Modern sanitation was inevitably a late development since very few villages had piped water supplies, but it is interesting to note that Henry Roberts's 1848 design for model cottages contained water-closets even if only with outside access, whereas when Prince Albert and Roberts designed a pair of model cottages for the 1851 Exhibition water-closets were provided with internal access, not only on the ground floor, but upstairs as well. These cottages were reconstructed at Kennington in south London after the Exhibition, where they still stand.[26]

However it is unlikely that many villages had piped water before the twentieth century, and it was in the industrial villages close to towns that progress was most rapid. In 1859 Akroyden was supplied with water and gas, and drainage was by 'sanitary tubes'. Bathrooms were still unknown, but an interesting variation on the usual tin tub before the fire was provided at Bourneville (*c*. 1895) where a sunken bath was built in the kitchen floor in front of the range. When required its cover was removed and it could be filled from large kettles warmed on the range.[27]

Generally speaking, model villages almost certainly provided above-average accommodation by the standards of the time, and usually supplied it at an artificially low rent as well. If the quality of the housing seems inadequate today that is merely a reflection of how much the general standard of living (and its associated expectations) have risen since Victoria's time.

The greater wealth (and often the greater needs) of industrialists enabled them to pioneer some of the improvements in housing standards and introduce them before they became practical in agricultural villages; but conversely it may have been the latter which inspired some industrialists to provide housing for their workers in the context of a village or garden suburb rather than in the densely packed urban tradition.

An interesting example of the industrial village approach is provided by Street in Somerset, now a small town virtually attached to Glastonbury, but for many years a model industrial village. Street is the home of the shoemaking firm of C. & J. Clark Ltd, one of the largest shoe manufacturers in Britain. This is very much a family firm, founded by Quaker farmers in 1825 when Street had a population of around 800 people. Shoemaking was at that time a cottage industry which provided employment for people living in Street and a number of surrounding villages. Clarks, however, were so successful with their shoes that it became necessary to bring in machinery to meet the expanding demand of the 1850s, and by 1861 the firm was producing 208,000 pairs of shoes a year. The population of Street was then 1,900. of whom practically all worked for Clarks. By 1901 the population had reached 4,000 (and shoe production 800,000 pairs), but Street still retained its village character.[28]

The Clarks had built their factory in 1857 right next to their own house in the main street, and there it still stands, though considerably enlarged. From the beginning they decided to provide housing for their workpeople, and the roads and houses were carefully planned and laid out to ensure that ample gardens and recreation space were left. The local lias stone (called blue, but actually a light grey) provided an excellent building material, and the company houses were built in a modified vernacular similar to that which is so attractively displayed in nearby towns and villages like Somerton and Compton Dundon.[29]

Although now too big to be regarded any longer as a village, Street yet retains the physical limits and the small community atmosphere which the more widely celebrated industrial garden suburbs, like Bourneville, Port Sunlight, and New Earswick, have to some extent lost because of their proximity to large cities. The outward sprawl of Birmingham, Birkenhead, and York has threatened them with encirclement and absorption, and although they have managed to retain a semi-rural atmosphere the village community aspect has inevitably tended to wither. However, all these industrial communities (Street included) share with traditional model villages the overriding influence (though not always the dominance) of one employer family. Lord Leverhulme at Port Sunlight clearly revelled in his paternalistic role, though the other three, the Cadburys at Bournville, the Rowntrees at New Earswick, and the Clarks at Street (all Quakers), were more concerned to try to reduce this aspect of their role so as not to induce hostile reactions amongst their employees. For the feeling of resentment at obligation, which can arise even towards the most beneficent of patrons, has always been the most troublesome fly in the ointment of the model village. With this aspect of the subject we will conclude this chapter.

In a situation where a landlord was providing the housing and, as frequently happened in model villages, other amenities as well, such as allotments, sports grounds, clubhouses ('reading rooms' as they were often called), and generally a well-organized and pleasant environment, he would inevitably expect to receive the gratitude, respect, and obedience of his tenants. Equally inevitably they were inclined to feel a sense of being manipulated and a loss of self-respect. This feeling was no doubt accentuated in cases where the landlord disapproved of public houses (as many did), or expected regular attendance at church (as Lady Wantage did). At Selworthy in west Somerset Lady Acland provided red cloaks for the old-age pensioners to wear. This may have made the rural scene more charming, but must also have added to the feeling of diminished independence.[30]

All these issues were ventilated in a pointed way in relation to the Lockinge estate in an article which appeared in the Liberal *Daily News* of 25 September 1891. It was written by a 'special commissioner' who paid a visit to the estate, and appeared under the title 'Arcadia Realised', together with Lord Wantage's reply. The main points are given in the following quotations.

> One of the most interesting and instructive scenes of rural life in England may be found in the villages of Lockinge and Ardington. . . . I went over yesterday because two or three years back I understood that the owner of this vast estate was going to crown and complete the remarkable little social system he has created here, by admitting his people to a share in the profits of his farming, and I wished to learn a little about the result of it.

'These villages of Ardington and Lockinge' the special commissioner went on,

> are well worthy of a visit. Seen in the early summer especially, as I saw them on a former occasion, they strike one as quite a little rural paradise. The estate is beautifully timbered; the cottages with their ornamental eaves and pointed gables, their fanciful chimney-stacks and pretty porches overgrown with ivy and roses, their grassy slopes and lawns and shrubs and flower-beds, all present innumerable points of view with which the artist would be enraptured. Every villager has, or may have, his allotment. There is an admirable reading room and a public house in charge of a salaried manager who has no interest whatever in pushing the sale of drink, but who is especially required to provide soup in winter, and tea and coffee and other non-toxicants at all times. There is a first-rate co-operative store, with commodious premises, at which the people can get all the necessaries of life, clothes, grocery, bread, meat, and provisions, on profit-sharing terms. The bakery is a beautiful little place, with patent ovens and the newest machinery. In addition to all this, over a hundred villagers are employed in municipal workshops, so to speak – shops fitted with all kinds of the latest machinery and the best appliances – saw-mills, carpenters' shops, blacksmiths' shops, painters' shops, wheelwrights' shops – all for the building and repairing and general maintenance of the property on the estate. There are two churches and an excellent school. In short, it is a little self-contained world in which nobody is idle, nobody is in absolute want, in which there is no squalor or hunger, while in the midst of it all is the great house of Lockinge, the beautiful home of Lord and Lady Wantage, always ready to play the part of benevolent friends to all who need their help, and who indeed, by all accounts, seem sincerely desirous of promoting the happiness and well-being of their people. The regular pay of the labourers on the estate is not higher than elsewhere. I understand that it was a shilling or so higher at one time, and that in consequence Lord Wantage has the very cream of the labourers in that part of the world, but that it was reduced to ten-shillings a week when the profit-sharing scheme was promulgated the expectation being that this reduction would be more than counterbalanced by the dividend that would be distributed when the farm accounts were made up.

Having found so much to praise at Ardington and Lockinge the special commissioner turned to what he thought 'radically rotten and bad':

> The whole system of things here is another illustration of that 'model' village life which is merely another name for social and political death. Lord Wantage is not to be attacked. He stands high in the esteem of all his neighbours and friends – unless maybe some of the tradesmen in

> the little town of Wantage, who are naturally angry with co-operative supply stores – and he has most laudably and consistently carried his Conservative principles into action. Materially, the result on the face of it is delightful and as a means of keeping the control and management of the people by the aristocracy nothing could possibly be better. But for all the purposes of political life and social progress and human development it is utterly bad. Lord Wantage has done for the people, in the true spirit of benevolent Toryism, what the people ought to be able to do for themselves – not individually, of course, but collectively and unitedly, and by their own sturdy independent and manly effort. I don't know what Lord Wantage's personal wish may be with regard to the voting power of his own people but I am sure that those people themselves have no idea whatever that they are free electors. 'Any politicians here?' I asked an old man as I walked up the road with him through Lockinge. 'What's them?' said the man with a puzzled air. 'Politicians,' I bawled, thinking the old man was a little deaf or very stupid – 'Politicians – you know what politicians are.' 'Be-em animals they goes out to shoot?' said the old fellow. Then I saw the waggish twinkle of his eyes that told me plainly enough he was only making a fool of me. He knew very well what politicians were, but he wasn't going to talk about such matters at Lockinge, and I couldn't induce him to. All around I heard Ardington and this village spoken of as a political dead sea, in which no public opinion ever was known to manifest itself. Nobody would say that Lord Wantage was a man to exercise any improper influence on his people; but he is a strong Tory, has been a member of the Tory government, his agents are Tories, and he owns all the land and houses, and can give or take away employment. I could not find anybody who knew of a political meeting having been held in these places. I heard it rumoured that there was one man who dared avow himself a Liberal, but I couldn't find him. 'O yes, Sir', said a woman in the place, 'they all votes Lord Wantage's way, of course. It wouldn't do for em to go again 'im.'

And according to the *Daily News* reporter, many of the amenities of Lord Wantage's villages were accompanied by irritating restrictions on individual freedom:

> I am assured that the admirable little public house in Ardington is to a great extent a failure, because the men find that they are not free to talk there, and that whatever they say is liable to be carried by the birds to the agent's or bailiff's ears. The people are managed and governed and controlled without the least voice in their public and collective affairs, and, though they undoubtedly have strong opinions on certain matters, they dare not give expression to them. For instance, the people have allotments for growing their own vegetables, but they must not

keep a pig. They have flower gardens in front of their cottages; if they don't keep them in order the bailiff will be down upon them. A labourer doesn't quite like his cottage; there is no possibility of shifting without the bailiff's consent and arrangement. 'They daren't blow their noses over at Ardington without the bailiff's leave,' said a labourer in the neighbourhood. The people control nothing, have no part whatever in anything like public life, nor any voice in matters directly affecting their own welfare. . . .

For their village stores the men ought to subscribe their own capital, pay interest, if at all, into their own coffers, and pocket the profit of the whole business. The management would, of course, be in the hands of the people themselves, who would elect their own officers and control their own affairs. Whatever advantage there might be would be public advantage, and it would all be consistent with everybody's perfect freedom and independence. There need be no fear of anybody, no cringing to agents, no concealment of opinions – absolutely nothing inconsistent with free, individual, manly life and sturdy citizenship.

To the Editor of the *Daily News*

Sir, . . . It is not my desire or intention to enter into any controversy; but I feel it would be unfortunate if some of the systems in operation on my estates, which your commissioner describes, were to be discredited by erroneous statements which would have the effect of discouraging their adoption elsewhere.

A correspondent of yours who signs himself 'Lockinge' makes many and varied complaints on behalf of the labourers of this district. Among these the allegation that the 'bonus' system has caused universal dissatisfaction among the labourers on this estate can only have a misleading and mischievous effect. In spite of what this correspondent says, I strongly (after experience of some years) recommend the system as an incentive to industry, and as conducive to a widening of interest on the part of the labourers in the prosperity of the farm on which they work. The bonus is, as your commissioner points out, given over and above the regular wages paid to farm labourers on this estate, which are in no way affected by it, and which rise and fall according to the fluctuation of supply and demand. It is not intended that the bonus system should be worked on strictly profit-sharing principles, which at present involves considerable practical working difficulties, but which further experience may possibly overcome. But the amount of bonus given is dependent on the profit realised. Certain farms of mine, which till recently made no profits, and consequently gave no bonus, have since last year paid their way, and have yielded a bonus, which I hope may be gradually increased in amount as the farm profits improve. The enforcement of sanitary regulations naturally falls upon the landlord, whether he happens to hold town or country property, and the insurance of healthy conditions by means of estate rules must in some cases override other considerations. The convenience of a pig-sty close to the cottage back-door is more than counter-balanced by the contamination of the neighbouring well. But it by no means follows that, because a pig-sty is not allowed close to a cottage, the cottager is forbidden to have one elsewhere. The allotment is the most suitable place for a pig-sty, and on this estate every man, can, if he wishes, have one put up at cost price, and removed at his convenience. Allotments should, where possible, be in near proximity to the village. Such is the case on this estate, and the proof that they are not 'failures' is that the demand for them is such that none are ever vacant. The management of the public house is so well described by your commissioner that I need say no more about it, except to observe that the sole restrictions enforced are such as the law of the land imposes, namely, those restricting the supply of liquor when men are in a state of drunkenness. The co-operative stores established in these villages distribute the whole of the profits among their customers, being worked on what is known as the Rochdale co-operative system. This mode of distribution was adopted, after full consideration, in preference to another plan, also on the Rochdale principle, which disposes of the profit in the shape of dividends, among the shareholders. But when there are shareholders who take these dividends, the money returned to the customers on their purchases is to that extent diminished, and this consideration has guided the managers of these stores in their adoption of a system which is working very satisfactorily.

It has been said in your columns that it is easy to draw pleasant pictures of the condition of the agricultural worker under the care of a beneficent landlord. But why assume that such a condition can only be purchased at the expense of freedom to think and act for himself? The fact that we live in democratic days is no reason for disparaging and discouraging the legitimate influence landlords may exercise over their neighbours and tenants by helpful supervision and by friendly interest in their affairs which ought not, and which do not, interfere with the freedom of speech and liberty of action which are the right of all alike, of labourers as well as landlords.

I am, Sir, your obedient servant,

Wantage

Lockinge House, Wantage, Berks, October 3 [1891].[31]

These two quotations provide such an excellent summary of the conflicting contemporary views of model villages that further comment is hardly necessary; except to point out that the economic advantages of residing in one could be very real. Those who wished to maintain a more independent and self-reliant way of life had a high a price to pay.

In conclusion it should be noted that model villages (both rural and industrial) had a far wider influence than their limited numbers would imply: for if a few landlords could aspire to remodelling a whole village, there must have been hundreds who were inspired by the example to tackle the housing problem on a smaller scale. New cottages were built to ampler and more convenient standards, and older cottages, which might otherwise have been neglected, were refurbished or extended. Thus was the influence of the model villages filtered through the whole of the Victorian countryside.

Notes

1 See Havinden, 1966, for a general history of Lockinge and the Wantage estate.
2 See Darley, 1975, for an excellent and wide-ranging discussion of the many types of model village.
3 See Thompson, 1963, *passim*.
4 Cited by Darley, 1975, 8.
5 Price, 1794–8, cited by Cooper, 1967, 1454.
6 Pevsner, 1958, 468–9.
7 Darley, 1975, 45–7.
8 *Country Life*, 10 December 1904, 881–2.
9 Holderness, 1972, *passim*.
10 Allen, 1846, *passim*.
11 Hadfield, 1970, *passim*.
12 Boyson, 1970, 115–40.
13 Holroyd, 1871, *passim*.
14 Wilson, 1954, I, 142–58.
15 Darley, 1975, 30.
16 Cooper, 1967, 1456.
17 Pevsner, 1953, 129–31.
18 Cooper, 1967, 1456.
19 Darley, 1975, 67.
20 Havinden, 1966, 105–11.
21 Darley, 1975, 92–4.
22 Havinden, 1966, 54.
23 ibid., 68.
24 ibid., 69.
25 ibid., 95–6.
26 Darley, 1975, 45–6.
27 ibid., 67, 70.
28 Clark, 1975, *passim*.
29 Little, 1974, 129–34.
30 Acland, 1976, 9.
31 Havinden, 1966, 113–18.

3

Country towns

C. W. Chalkin

> The agricultural and pastoral character of the people upon whom the town depended for its existence was shown by the class of objects displayed in the shop windows. Scythes, reap-hooks, sheep-shears, bill-hooks, spades, mattocks, and hoes at the ironmonger's; beehives, butter-firkins, churns, milking stools and pails, hay-rakes, field-flagons, and seed-lips at the cooper's; cart-ropes and plough-harness at the saddler's; carts, wheelbarrows, and mill-gear at the wheelwright's and machinist's; horse embrocations at the chemist's; at the glover's and leather-cutter's, hedging-gloves, thatcher's knee-caps, ploughman's leggings, villager's patterns and clogs.
>
> Thomas Hardy, *The Mayor of Casterbridge*[1]

> 'Will you tell me what is sold in this general market?' 'All sorts of things. Anyone may have a stall for boots if he likes as long as he pays the toll. There are a good many people who sell crockery, and then there are butchers, and fishmongers, and those people who sell anything in the nature of provisions.'
>
> Report of the Royal Commission on Market Rights and Tolls 1888, concerning Newbury[2]

Nineteenth century urban historians have tended to give their attention to London, the metropolitan industrial and commercial cities of the Midlands and the north, and the lesser manufacturing centres that were rising in their wake. In view of their importance, size, and pace of growth this is natural enough. Yet the several hundred market towns and small regional centres in the countryside, whose basic role was to provide a variety of services for the farming communities, are equally worthy of study. In the Victorian period, as in earlier centuries, the country town was the basic English urban type.

Most of these country towns were essentially of local importance. Through their markets and fairs, a growing variety of shops, a wide range of crafts, and a few professional men, they were service centres for a rural hinterland of perhaps no more than three or four miles in radius. Many of them had some cottage industries, and some had workshops and small factories; if they lay on the coast, fishing, seaborne trade, or summer visitors provided an additional livelihood. A minority of country towns were small regional centres; in comparison with the average market town they had many more different tradesmen and craftsmen, larger markets, and their shops stocked a wider range of goods. Some had a sphere of influence covering several market towns: in addition to their local trade and commercial links with other parts of England, their regional importance was often symbolized by an administrative function as a county town or as the headquarters of a see of a diocese. As in the smaller country towns industry was sometimes an important subsidiary means of livelihood.

There was thus some variation in the size of the country towns. At the opening of the Victorian period the typical market town had a population of between 1,000 and 4,000. As an example let us look first at the towns of the western part of Sussex in 1841. There were four small inland market towns, Arundel (population of the parish 2,624), Petworth (3,364), Midhurst (1,536), and Steyning (1,495). The parishes of Petworth and to a lesser extent Arundel and Steyning had a considerable rural acreage and the population of the market towns alone was probably much smaller. Worthing was primarily a seaside resort, but Littlehampton combined the function of small market town, port, and seaside resort. In the north-west of the county the town of Horsham, the major trading centre in the western Weald, had less than 5,000 people (parish population 5,765). Chichester (8,512) was the regional centre of west Sussex, an important market town and see of the diocese of Chichester. All the country towns differed from the villages in their hinterlands in that the majority of the occupied inhabitants of the latter were directly involved in agriculture as farmers or labourers, and that the trades and crafts in the towns were far more varied and specialized. The likely size of the hinterlands of the market towns may be illustrated by the case of Midhurst. The market towns of Petersfield and Haslemere in adjoining counties lay eight miles to the north and west respectively; Chichester lay ten miles to the south, and Petworth only six miles to the east. The difference between the commercial importance of a town such as Midhurst or Arundel and, say, Horsham was visible partly in its occupations. While there is no evidence that the markets at Midhurst or Arundel were of more than local importance, according to *The Post Office Directory of the Six Home Counties* (1845) at Horsham 'large quantities of corn and poultry are sold here for the London supply'. In the same directory 109 tradesmen, craftsmen, and professional people were listed for Midhurst, representing fifty-one different occupations; Horsham had 235 people listed, representing ninety-one occupations. Horsham clearly served a bigger rural hinterland than did Midhurst.

As a second and to some extent contrasting example, Oxfordshire in 1841 may be chosen. Oxford, with 30,000 people, was an important regional centre, linked to the Midlands and London by water. It was a county town and see of the diocese, with the university providing an important additional livelihood for its inhabitants. With one exception the nine or ten other urban centres in the county were small. Unlike the towns of western Sussex nearly all had some manufacturing in various states of prosperity, in addition to the agricultural processing industries to be found in all country towns. At Burford (population 1,644), where the market was held on a Saturday,

> the making of saddles, and a considerable trade in malt and wool, that formerly flourished, have much declined: this, added to the diversion of the line of road, which now avoids the town, instead of passing through it as before, has reduced it from a flourishing condition to a state of comparative poverty.[3]

The neighbouring market town of Witney (3,419), seven miles away, was exceptional in the presence of an important and flourishing local industry, blanket making, the greatest source of employment in the town. In 1852 it was said that every year about 93,000 blankets were made, the six chief manufacturers in the town using weekly 120 packs of wool.[4] At Charlbury (1,526 in 1851) it was reported in 1852 that the weekly market was almost in disuse, but was hoped to improve after the opening of a railway. It was still a minor trading centre: 'owing to its being surrounded by about twenty villages within a circuit of a few miles, a considerable trade is carried on at Charlbury'. Glove making was an important employment: 'here is the largest glove manufactory in the county'.[5] Probably, apart from Oxford, only Banbury had importance as a centre for the supply of goods and the collection of agricultural produce greater than that of the typical market town. Its population in 1841 was 6,753. In 1843 there were said to be 'one hundred and forty places within a circuit of ten miles' for which Banbury was a 'metropolis'. Plush-weaving was a special minor industry, in about 1850 a steam-powered factory for worsted and mohair spinning was built, employing fifty workers, and shoemaking served more than purely local needs.[6] Altogether in the market towns of Oxfordshire in the mid-nineteenth century, as in some neighbouring counties, textile and other manufactures were an important means of livelihood.

Some country towns grew rapidly in the Victorian period (though not at the pace of the majority of towns in the big industrial regions); others practically stood still. Some prospered as better communications brought by the railways attracted the agricultural trade of a wider area, or with the development of local industry; others stagnated as the population of the rural hinterland ceased to grow, or even declined, as the developing railway network passed them by and drew trade away to neighbouring market towns or regional centres, or as existing cottage industry faded in the face of factory competition. Thus in Sussex Horsham's population more than doubled between 1841 and 1901 (5,765 to 12,994). With the help of favourable rail communications its role as the major marketing and agricultural processing centre in the western Weald expanded; in the 1890s it was noted for its important corn, poultry, and cattle markets, corn mills, malthouses, breweries, iron and brass foundries, and coach factories.[7] In contrast, the trading centres of Midhurst, Petworth, Arundel, and Steyning hardly grew at all. Steyning, as Kelly's directories indicate, was the most thriving of them with, in 1891, two breweries, a fatstock sale on alternate Wednesdays, and a corn and cattle market on alternate Mondays; it grew from 1,495 in 1841 to 1,752 in 1901. The population of Petworth parish decreased from 3,364 to 2,503, and that of Midhurst rose by barely a hundred (1,536 to 1,650); and while they retained their function as minor shopping centres, their markets had disappeared by the early 1900s.[8] In mid-Sussex important rail communications helped to create a new town, Haywards Heath, with, by 1891, an important agricultural trade, 'the largest cattle sale in Sussex being held here'.[9]

The pattern of urban development in Oxfordshire, as in other counties in the south Midlands, was influenced by the differing fortunes of the local industries which had been so important in the economies of the market towns in the early nineteenth century. By 1900 Oxford with its 50,000 people had been transformed into much more than a county town. Banbury (10,012 in 1901) had grown slowly, helped by good rail communications and the consequent development of the manufacture of agricultural implements and engines.[10] With the exception of Chipping Norton, the population of the other market towns had not increased at all owing to the slow decline of the neighbouring agricultural population which they served and the stagnation or decline of the little cottage or workshop industries, such as the making of gloves, lace, and shoes.

Victorian England inherited three types of market from previous centuries, the general retail markets for the sale of many sorts of perishable provisions and cheap household goods, corn markets, and livestock markets. The fortunes of individual markets of all three types fluctuated during the course of the later nineteenth century. Some gained trade, others lost it. A few disappeared altogether, particularly general and corn markets, as trade was diverted to neighbouring towns or was carried on by other means. Some new markets were created as a result of local initiative, perhaps encouraged by the arrival of favourable rail communications. Many retail markets continued to prosper. In 1888 when the Royal Commission on Market Rights was investigating the market at Market

Drayton, Shropshire, it found that farmers' wives were continuing to bring provisions for sale to the market place as they had done for centuries.[11]

Nevertheless, the number and importance of these retail markets was declining. Some country towns lost them altogether, in others little trade was done. Village and town shops were absorbing more and more of the business in perishable foodstuffs formerly done in the markets. As consumption grew there was increasing need for more regular outlets for farm produce than the weekly market could provide, and hawkers as well as shopkeepers helped to satisfy this growing demand. In 1888 the lessee of the Helston, St Austell, and Penrhyn markets in Cornwall complained to an assistant commissioner: '[Helston] market is decreasing very much, the trade being diverted to the shops; in fact in most of the country towns the market has gone . . . every village has its butcher's shop and vegetable shop.'[12] In many towns hawkers with vegetables, fruit, poultry, and eggs toured the streets every day, though not every market was much affected by them. According to an assistant commissioner who visited Hereford market in 1888: 'there is no doubt tradespeople do more and more go out with their carts, and a great many markets that I have been to suffered from it, but I do not find that this market has'.[13] In some towns, such as Guildford in Surrey, shops selling perishable foodstuffs tended to cater for the well-to-do, while the working class continued to patronize the market.[14]

The numerous corn exchanges created up and down the country are a witness to the fact that market trading in corn (generally by sample) remained active and their importance is supported by contemporary evidence.[15] In fact, in many towns dealing in corn, trading outside markets tended to limit profits from market tolls. Much corn was sold in inns, in open streets, or by direct conveyance from farm gate to mill. At Banbury two corn exchanges were erected in 1857 as a result of competition by rival companies. One was still in use in 1888 with about forty corn stands let to dealers at £1 a year, but it was not a financial success because much dealing was still done in the yard of the Red Lion Inn in the High Street and later at the Crown Inn in Bridge Street.[16]

Livestock markets, involving particularly lean and fat cattle and sheep but also horses and pigs, were perhaps the most important form of market trading in the Victorian period. By the 1880s and 1890s they had tended to absorb the great annual fairs in cattle, sheep, and horses, leaving fairs, if they were held at all, for merrymaking and, still in many towns, for the traditional hiring of farm servants. At Banbury in 1888 fortnightly market sales were said to average 1,000 sheep and 1,200 cattle.[17] Many cattle markets were created or developed as a result of new facilities which captured trade from neighbouring towns, or because railways replaced the traditional transport 'on the hoof'. In 1888, for example, the livestock market at Sevenoaks was said to be not so important as it had been formerly. One reason was that in 1849 the neighbouring town of Tonbridge, in addition to its existing market, had set up a second cattle market on the third Tuesday in each month, which competed with Sevenoaks' existing Tuesday market; another cause was the construction of the South Eastern Railway:

> Sheep from Romney Marsh and that district were brought to this market by hundreds; they came here through Tonbridge instead of stopping at Tonbridge to be sold as they do now. Instead of sending sheep to Sevenoaks market they now send them to Ashford or Tonbridge for dispatch to London by rail.[18]

Despite the varying fortunes of individual markets up and down England, market day remained by far the most important day of the week for most country towns. This may be seen in the large number of carriers that poured into the towns on their market days. The Ditchling, Sussex, carrier transported 'pork from farms in Wivelsfield, hides for Lewes tannery, rabbits on poles, vegetables by the bushel, butter in chocolate boxes, baskets of laundry, razors, scissors, and ploughshares for sharpening, also numerous parcels, contents unknown'.[19] Most, though not all, of the services were on market day. At Melton Mowbray, Leicestershire, a town of nearly 6,000 people in the 1880s, four-fifths of the services run to the town by carriers in no less than sixty neighbouring villages were on the single market day, Tuesday.[20]

In addition to the markets, the towns served the surrounding countryside by means of their various crafts, distributive trades, and professional men. Towns which lacked an important industry had a relatively similar occupational pattern. A typical example is Ashby de la Zouch, a Leicestershire market town with just under 4,000 people in 1861 (see table 3.1). Particularly in the smaller towns those earning a livelihood directly from the land – farmers, market gardeners, and numerous agricultural labourers – who tended to live near the edge of the built-up area comprised a significant minority of the working population, perhaps 10, 15, or 20 per cent. Another large group were the domestic servants. The numbers of those working in transport (such as railway workers, carriers, canal boat hands) or in services (such as hairdressers or chimney sweeps), and general labourers, were smaller but still significant. Yet it was not uncommon for the various craftsmen (with their apprentices and skilled assistants), retailers, and professional people to comprise about half the working population.

By far the most numerous group were the craftsmen. Many of the master craftsmen retailed the goods they produced in their own shops. So many goods which are today supplied from a distance, typically from a factory, were made locally. This was particularly true of clothing and

Table 3.1 The occupational structure of Ashby de la Zouch according to the 1861 census (individuals)

	%
crafts	35
domestic servants	15
trades	13
agricultural workers	9
services	6.5
labourers	6
professions	5
innkeepers	4
independent	3.5
farmers and graziers	1.5
clerical workers	1.5

Source: Page, 1974, 86.

shoes, always important in providing work for townspeople. For example, in 1857 at Tadcaster, a market town in the Vale of York, of 2,516 inhabitants, 99 people, or just about one-third of the 297 masters, journeymen, and apprentices working at all the skilled crafts, were tailors, shoemakers and cordwainers, and dressmakers. Much of the work was done, as one might expect, for the inhabitants of the neighbouring parishes. An 80-year-old lady living in Tadcaster in 1970 recalled how her shoemaker grandfather in his old age thought nothing of walking a twelve-mile round trip to deliver his shoe repairs to customers in the villages.[21] If there was no tailor in a country parish, a man might travel from a nearby country town with made-to-measure or ready-made clothes. One tailor and draper from Stowmarket, Suffolk, used to travel round villages at harvest time when the men had received extra pay, collecting orders which he executed in the family workshop.[22] Many of the tailors in the country towns were also drapers, and sold ready-made clothing in shops. This was the case at Tadcaster, which had 2 hat manufacturers, 5 stay-makers, 5 milliners, and 3 bonnet-makers. Another numerous occupational group in all the country towns was the building trades. At Tadcaster there were 109 people in building and allied occupations. They included 38 joiners, carpenters, and cabinet-makers, 19 stonemasons, 11 bricklayers, 12 house painters, 9 sawyers, 4 plasterers, 2 plumbers and glaziers, and several men in brick- and tile-making. It was not uncommon for a few master craftsmen in these trades each to employ up to a dozen or even a score of skilled workmen as well as apprentices, and to turn their hand to a variety of work. In 1851 John Rodwell of Tadcaster was employing six men and two apprentices. Seven years earlier a local directory described him as a 'cabinet maker, upholsterer, builder, turner, picture frame maker, undertaker etc.', and he announced as his speciality 'all kinds of fancy work and needlework mounted. Cane and rush bottom chairs manufactured and repaired.' In an economy which remained dependent on horse-drawn vehicles for local transport, saddlers, blacksmiths, and wheelwrights were naturally numerous in both town and country. Tadcaster had 10 people working at the saddler's craft, 6 wheelwrights, and 3 smithies employing 11 men. In addition all towns had an assortment of craftsmen who did not fall into any of the categories so far mentioned. They included braziers, turners, clockmakers, coopers, curriers, and many others.

In every town in the mid-nineteenth century those working at crafts, many of whom sold their wares direct to the customer, greatly outnumbered the inhabitants who were merely retailers. The most common tradesmen included butchers, grocers, and drapers, and every town had a variety of more specialized retailers. Among the 4,000 inhabitants of Tonbridge, Kent, in 1851 were numerous butchers, beersellers, grocers, and drapers, and there were also greengrocers, fishmongers, milkmen, coalmen, and clothiers. The more specialized tradesmen included stationers, a bookseller, a wine merchant, and as many as four tea dealers.[23] A special group were the publicans. In Banbury there was one for every 110 of the population in 1851, and one for every 131 in 1871.[24]

In the later nineteenth century it is likely that the number of shops, shopkeepers, and shop workers grew faster than the population. By the 1880s, if not before, shops were taking over trade in perishable goods previously handled by retail markets in some towns. Furthermore, the growing volume and variety and cheapness of factory-made goods restricted the work of craftsmen–retailers and increased the sales of those tradesmen who were just shopkeepers. Towards the end of the nineteenth century more and more factory-made boots, watches, and clothes were being sold. New types of shop were appearing in the country towns, reflecting the widening range of goods available and new tastes on the part of more well-to-do customers. In 1898 Huntingdon (population 4,349 in 1891) had a dealer in antique furniture, a firm of photographers, and an agent and maker of bicycles. Rising real incomes among the mass of the population led to the appearance of multiple shops particularly in footwear and provisions: thus Huntingdon in 1898 had its Freeman, Hardy & Willis, and its International Tea Company.[25]

As the volume of machine-made goods manufactured outside the district grew, the number of craftsmen in the country towns began to decline.[26] In Devon the number of shoemakers was nearly 6,000 in 1871, but had fallen to 3,000 by 1901.[27] Nearly all the traditional crafts of the country town still existed at the beginning of the twentieth century, but they were drawing increasingly on the factory or large-scale industry to supply half-finished goods – iron axles, saddlers' ironmongery, lead piping, sawn planks, and sewing thread – and employment opportunities for young townsmen in these trades were becoming more and more limited.

Professional services were also an important feature of every country town. Apart from the clergy, Anglican and Nonconformist, there were various teachers, solicitors, medical practitioners, bankers, accountants, and surveyors, among others. Thus Tadcaster in 1851 had 5 clergy, comprising the vicar and his curate, 2 Wesleyan ministers and 1 Inghamite, 4 doctors, 2 governesses, 14 teachers at various types of school (4 men and 10 women), 4 solicitors, 3 opticians, 3 bookkeepers, an inland revenue officer, an auctioneer, 2 artist painters, and a professor of music.[28] Although relatively few in number, only a tiny proportion of the occupied population, the professions were an essential part of the functions of the country town.

There was some industry in nearly every country town. Often it merely comprised the processing of agricultural produce by millers, maltsters, brewers, and tanners. But many country towns made agricultural equipment, machinery and engines, or manufactured goods with no direct connection with agriculture, such as woollens, lace, gloves, straw plaits, or furniture. In coastal towns fishing, boat-building, and sometimes the provision of accommodation for summer visitors, provided additional employment.

Among the industries closely linked to agriculture, milling had always been ubiquitous. In the middle of the nineteenth century nearly every town, however small, had its windmill or watermill run by a miller and one or two assistants; the larger towns and those in fertile corn-growing districts which supplied London or one of the industrial regions often had several windmills and watermills. Where grain supplies and demand were sufficiently large some relatively big enterprises emerged. For example, mid-nineteenth-century Gloucester, in the centre of a grain-producing area, supplied increasing quantities of flour to industrial south Wales. In addition to its many small windmills and watermills, there were a number of large mills, sometimes owned in conjunction with other businesses. In the late 1830s a man named Healing took over the Abbey Mills in Gloucester, operating them as well as the Quay Mills at Tewkesbury and Cox's Mill at Evesham, the total output being about 700 sacks of flour a week. In the 1860s he increased his business by building a steam mill at Tewkesbury and adding further capacity until his output was over 3,000 sacks a week.[29] But with the increased use of steampower, machinery, and the growing reliance on imported wheat entering the country through the great ports, many of the small watermills and windmills in the agricultural regions were abandoned or converted to other uses. Bridlington, a market town, port, and resort on the Yorkshire coast, had no fewer than seven windmills and three watermills in 1853. But only one watermill and two windmills appear to have been still grinding corn at the beginning of the twentieth century. One watermill had been converted for the manufacture of manure, and the third had become by 1882 a steam saw mill.[30]

In the early nineteenth century every country town had at least one malthouse to supply the local brewers. Some towns in barley-growing areas or with access to imported barley, and with good water communications to large markets, were well known for numerous maltings, such as Newark on Trent in Nottinghamshire or Saffron Walden in Essex. Later many small malthouses became disused because local breweries obtained their malt from their own malthouses, or because they lay distant from rail communications suitable for the carriage of malt to large urban markets. In 1877 Thaxted in Essex witnessed 'huge maltings and granaries falling into decay. To such a state of inactivity does seven miles from a railway station reduce a once thriving borough.'[31] At Newark, on the other hand, the railways gave access to both coal and distant markets; many more malthouses were built and several large businesses emerged.[32]

During the course of the later nineteenth century the more successful breweries tended to become bigger as premises were enlarged, plant was modernized, amalgamations took place, and public houses were bought. Typical of the more successful enterprises in its steady expansion was the brewing business of Henry Michell of Horsham (died 1874), whose diary over thirty-nine years recalls the major achievements of each year. When he began business in 1835 he brewed only about 400 quarters of malt in his first year and 600 quarters in his second year. In 1868 he brewed 3,075 quarters; in the interval he had acquired a new brewery (which he enlarged twice and adapted to the use of steam), a new malthouse, and a succession of public houses in the district. As early as 1837 he noted in his diary: 'this year I bought the Jolly Tanner at Staplefield Common for £400. . . . This proved a great bargain, as it has always yielded 5 per cent interest, besides a good beer trade.'[33] In Banbury, Hunt's brewery was enlarged between 1850 and 1866; after an additional partner joined the firm in 1872 his capital was used to buy sixty-four tied houses between 1874 and 1876. Four more breweries were taken over before 1900 and fifty public houses acquired in the 1890s.[34]

Yet another industry involving the processing of a farm product was the manufacture of leather. Nearly all country towns in the mid-nineteenth century had a tanyard drawing on cattle hides from local slaughterhouses, run by a tanner with perhaps five or six assistants. Usually, too, there was at least one master currier in the town who handled the final dressing and trimming of the leather. By the 1880s some of the small tanneries were closing down as local supplies of hides dwindled. Production tended to concentrate in the larger works using steampower, often relying on hides drawn from markets in the industrial cities or from abroad.[35]

Iron works were a feature of many country towns from the beginning of the nineteenth century. The typical small foundry of the 1830s made agricultural implements, general castings such as grates, range backs and pipes, and sometimes structural ironwork such as bridges. Later agricultural machinery, various types of engine, boilers and pumps, and sometimes railway equipment were made. Diversification often developed rapidly. In Buckingham the Castle Iron Foundry was set up in 1857 to make ploughs and harrows and other implements; within a few months it was producing a steam locomotive cultivator, and later it was making steam road cars. In 1860 the manager announced that he was taking orders for cars costing £180 and £200, and five years later he was building traction engines for hauling omnibuses.[36] In a few towns, generally those served with good rail communications, such as Banbury and Newark, large works emerged employing not tens but hundreds of men. In Banbury the largest works in the mid-nineteenth century, that of Bernhard Samuelson, had 27 workmen in 1846; by 1861 it was employing 380 men and boys.[37] The ever-widening demand for metal goods outside agriculture brought more and more firms into being in the more important country towns in the last decades of the century. In Essex firms were set up in the 1890s to make metal windows, accessories for moter and cycle trades, gramophones and pianos, and many other products.[38] Various textile industries were flourishing in the middle of the century in some of the predominantly agricultural regions, bringing much extra work to the country towns. Most of them were cottage industries, though in a few instances (as in the case of the silk manufacture of Essex) the work was carried on in small factories or workshops in the towns. For many, both employers and employed, these gave additional means of livelihood. Thus in the small market town of Castle Donington, Leicestershire (3,508 in 1841), where hosiery manufacture in the mid-nineteenth century was carried on in small factories, workshops, and particularly in the workers' homes, one hosiery manufacturer was also a farmer with 60 acres, another kept a grocer's shop, and a third had not only a general shop but was also a boot and shoemaker; rather later, in 1870, the publican who kept the King's Head in the Market Place was also a wholesale manufacturer of baby linen.[39] Some manufacturers employed women and girls in particular, providing additional income for families in which the head of the household worked at a craft or trade. The glove industry of Woodstock near Oxford was said to employ about 100 men and no less than 1,500 women in the district in 1852.[40]

During the course of the Victorian period the nature of employment in the textile industries sometimes changed, and in other cases disappeared altogether. Local factories using machinery gradually took over some of the processes previously done by outworkers, while cottagers continued to handle the remaining processes. At Woodstock in about 1900 the glove-making firm of R. & J. Pullman employed about 60 people in a factory and about 150 or 200 people in the neighbouring villages, presumably cottage workers engaged in sewing.[41] In other cases the local textile industry declined or disappeared as a result of competition from machine production in other regions or changes in fashion. In Bedfordshire the pillow lace industry, a cottage manufacture carried on in both town and country, was declining from the 1880s through the competition of production by machine.[42]

A few specialized industries developed in a particular country town and its district in response to the growth of a national demand for its products. Redditch in Worcestershire gained a national reputation for needles, Tonbridge in Kent for cricket balls. At High Wycombe in the early Victorian period the manufacture of chairs grew 'from a semi-rural craft of local fame to an industry of national importance'. The local products, with interwoven cane seats, were quite distinctive. In 1875 about seventy chair manufacturers employed nearly 700 householders in the district, and many young men, boys, girls, and women.[43]

The momentous economic and social changes of the Victorian period all left their mark on the country towns. A few, such as Lincoln, Reading, and Swindon, were transformed into important industrial or railway centres while retaining links with the surrounding countryside; a small number, particularly in the home counties, were swallowed up by the expansion of a large city. The majority altered slowly over the decades. In general the larger towns which were already of regional importance in the 1830s, or those which received the benefit of good rail links in the mid-nineteenth century, gained trade at the expense of the majority of country towns which were only of local importance. For many country towns market trading was ceasing to be so significant, and in a few it disappeared altogether. In most of them there was a greater variety of shops, and everywhere the range of goods sold in them was becoming larger. On the other hand, by the end of the century goods produced in other areas were slowly but surely restricting the work available to local craftsmen. So far as industry was concerned, cottage and small workshop industries were tending to decline or disappear, though with some exceptions; and, where manufacture survived in the town, it was tending to concentrate in larger works, mills, or factories. Yet in its essentials, as a trading centre for a primarily agrarian hinterland, the country town survived into the twentieth century.

Notes

1 Hardy [1886], 1974, 33.
2 BPP, 1888, LV, 74.
3 Lewis, 1840, 378.
4 *Victoria County History: Oxfordshire II*, 251.
5 Gardner, 1852, 637.
6 *Victoria County History: Oxfordshire X*, 13, 64–6.
7 Kelly, 1891, 2253.
8 Kelly, 1905, II, 509, 526.

9 Kelly, 1891, 2243.
10 *Victoria County History: Oxfordshire X*, 13, 67.
11 BPP, 1888, LVII, 481.
12 ibid., LIV, 169.
13 ibid., LIV, 124.
14 ibid., LV, 83.
15 ibid., LV, 174.
16 *Victoria County History: Oxfordshire X*, 60.
17 ibid.
18 BPP, 1888, LIV, 87–8.
19 Greening, 1971, 172.
20 Everitt, 1973, 232–5.
21 Brewster, 1970, 1–16.
22 Horn, 1976, 101.
23 Chalklin, 1975, 17.
24 Rogers, 1972, 225.
25 Kelly, 1898, 32.
26 Clapham, 1932, 125.
27 Horn, 1976, 101.
28 Brewster, 1970, 18–21.
29 Freeman, 1976, 84–5.
30 *Victoria County History: Yorkshire, East Riding II*, 56–7.
31 Booker, 1974, 74.
32 Cooper, 1971, 103–12.
33 Neale, 1974, 32, 38–40, 51, 56–7.
34 *Victoria County History: Oxfordshire X*, 86.
35 Jenkins, 1972, 61.
36 Elliott, 1975, 235–7.
37 *Victoria County History: Oxfordshire X*, 66–7.
38 Booker, 1974, 22.
39 Lee, 1956, 62.
40 *Victoria County History: Oxfordshire II*, 258.
41 ibid., 258.
42 *Victoria County History: Bedfordshire II*, 123.
43 Ashford, 1960, 290, 311.

4

The Victorian picture of the country

Rosemary Treble

In the Italian Renaissance the countryside – the landscape and the people in it – was a vehicle for the complex iconography of devotional art; to the French impressionists 500 years later, it provided material for an attempt at the pure perception of light, colour, and space. An almost infinite variety of approaches to nature lay between the two extremes and Victorian artists experimented with most of them, for paintings of rural subjects found ready buyers amongst urban patrons nostalgic for a countryside which many of them may only have left within a generation or less, and which represented a pastoral ideal disappearing beneath the onslaught of industrial development. The water-colourists have been exhaustively discussed during this century, above all by Martin Hardie,[1] and this brief introduction is biased towards the artists of the Royal Academy and towards the breakaway groups of the 1860s–1880s.

Pure landscape: naturalism and romanticism

Queen Victoria received the news of her accession on 20 June 1837 while *Arundel Mill and Castle* (plate 22) by John Constable (1776–1837) was showing posthumously in the Royal Academy summer exhibition. Around the same time Turner (1775–1851) was working on the last of his studies of Norham Castle, a place he had first painted in 1798 and which, in *Norham Castle, Sunrise* (plate 23), moved him to the furthest point of abstraction his landscape work achieved, surpassed only by the late studies of storms at sea. The two artists were then the grand old men of the English landscape tradition, but it was a tradition which had only a comparatively short life of less than a hundred years. Richard Wilson, Gainsborough, Stubbs, and the great water-colourists like Paul Sandby and Alexander Cozens created in the second half of the eighteenth century a new category of art, in which the elements of landscape played a major rather than a subordinate part, working on canvas what the landscape gardeners were working on the ground. The picturesque landscape challenged the academic supremacy of history painting and portraiture and made it possible for later artists to explore the full range of possibilities from the naturalism of Constable and the water-colourists to the near-abstract romanticism of Turner. All these developments were rooted in the seventeenth century, when the Dutch – Rembrandt, Van Goyen and Hobbema – and the French – above all Claude – provided the models for their English successors.[2]

The contrast between Constable's *Arundel* and Turner's *Norham* could not be more complete: the *Arundel* is densely worked with a classically structured three-dimensionality, complete with repoussoir (the foreground log), recessional diagonals, and the full apparatus of illusionistic landscape perspective. The *Norham* is an exploration of pure light, colour, and atmosphere, concerned far more with the luminous patches of palest yellow, blue, and green on the picture plane, the surface of the canvas itself, than with any reference to an actual location. Turner's revolutionary painting in both oil and watercolour took him so far beyond the contemporary aesthetic that, in the opinion of some modern writers, it has only recently been fully matched by the American abstract expressionists.[3] Certainly the immediate followers of Turner most often compared with him, James Baker Pyne (1800–70) and Clarkson Stanfield (1793–1867), were unable to pursue his experiments further. Pyne remained content with a golden Claudian glow, deployed to great effect in paintings like *Haweswater, from Waller Gill Force* (1850, Royal Holloway College), while Stanfield worked his landscapes and seascapes into imposing Academy machines, full of sound and fury but with an academic finish and admired by Ruskin as a worthy successor to the immortal Turner.

The search for truth in the representation of nature was the central motivation of both Turner and the Pre-Raphaelite Brotherhood, but the young Millais, Hunt, and Rossetti, following in the tracks of the German Nazarenes and of Ford Madox Brown and William Dyce, sought to capture the essence of nature by the minute representation of every visible element in the chosen scene, and totally rejected Turner's abstracted impressions. Ruskin championed both, Turner in the first volume of *Modern Painters* in 1843,[4] the Pre-Raphaelites from 1851 onwards, and initially saw no contradiction in his espousal of two such antithetical views of nature. The disintegration of the Brotherhood in the mid-1850s revealed its internal conflicts: at its best it had crystallized a radical movement in English art away from conservative and pedestrian academic views of the landscape; at its most idiosyncratic, the Pre-Raphaelite method, as practised by Hunt and Millais, slipped into a kind of mannered literalism that conveyed only the most specific and subjective experience of nature, rather than uncovering a new universal truth to nature as they had hoped. Millais' *Ophelia* (1851–2, Tate) is perhaps the prettiest as well as one of the clearest examples of this extreme position, which produced work of a novelty, honesty, and vitality that, as Allen Staley concludes in his major study *The Pre-Raphaelite Landscape*,[5] made it less important whether it succeeded than that it looked and tried.

The mainstream of landscape art, as with all other forms of painting and sculpture in England, was that shown at the Royal Academy each year. Here the walls, and consequently the viewing public's understanding of contemporary landscape art, were dominated in the early part of the reign by men like Thomas Creswick (1811–69), Frederick Lee (1798–1879), and Thomas Sidney Cooper (1803–1902), who represented the most conservative faction of a conservative Academy. The work of all three was repetitious in subject and composition (Cooper painted such quantities of livestock that he was known as 'Cow' Cooper), and lacked innovative talent, but they also possessed an enviable self-confidence, undoubted technical skill, and a genuine interest in the beauties of the English countryside that found a wide market amongst collectors from the most parvenu to the most discerning. Both Lee and Creswick collaborated with Cooper, who painted the cattle and sheep into many of their landscapes, while Cooper's own paintings ranged from the much repeated scenes of cattle grazing on his home ground of the Canterbury Meadows (like that at York, of 1858) to the majestically proportioned *The Halt on the Hills* (1847, Sheffield). Despite Cooper's protestations of disappointment with Paulus Potter's famous *Bull* at The Hague,[6] it is evident that he had been profoundly influenced by the Dutch treatment of animals in landscape during his years in Belgium and Holland in 1827–30, and the monumental forms of the animals in *The Halt on the Hills*, its foreground filled with a pyramidal composition of goats, sheep, and long-horned cattle, echoed in the shape of the mountains behind, the whole bathed in a warm golden light, illustrate Cooper at his most opulently arcadian. While Cooper was concerned with an expression of the nobility of the beast, Lee and Creswick produced generally tranquil transcriptions of the English landscape, composed under a limpid light and dotted with ruminating cattle or sheep, like Creswick's *Trentside* (1861, Royal Holloway College). Occasionally they would rise to more dramatic effects: it has been suggested for instance that Lee and Cooper's *The Chequered Shade* (plate 24), a modern and brilliant exercise in the manner of Hobbema's *The Avenue at Middleharnis*, was a riposte to Holman Hunt's *The Hireling Shepherd*, whose background is dominated by a similar avenue and sheep.[7]

The most popular of their younger successors was Benjamin Williams Leader (1831–1923), an artist who, as Staley points out, synthesized the precision of the Pre-Raphaelites with the subject matter of the academics and created the instantly recognizable Leader landscape, epitomized by *February Fill Dyke* (1881, Birmingham), highly finished and with a stylized, almost photographic, clarity. *In the Evening There shall be Light* (plate 25),[8] his Academy picture of 1882, was thought by his biographer[9] to be 'his finest production' and, though not well received by that year's reviews, the painting won for Leader a First Class Medal at the 1889 Paris Exposition Universelle, where a French critic commented that despite too much contrast and a throbbing colour scheme, it displayed a spiritual quality and a biblical solemnity.

Sentiment to social realism

One of the most powerful images of the Victorian countryside for the modern viewer, and for the Victorians themselves, was provided by scenes of cottage life, featuring rustic simplicity, sometimes in picturesque poverty, sometimes in virtuous and provident though rude comfort. This prettily sentimental view of country life was almost as mythical to its contemporaries as it is to the twentieth century, and seems to have owed its popularity as much to its unattainability as to the evident charm of the paintings it produced. The genre had its genesis in the Dutch seventeenth century with Ostade and Teniers, and in Spain with Murillo, was refined in Gainsborough's 'fancy pictures', and taken to its pre-Victorian limits by George Morland (1763–1804) and his successors, David Wilkie (1785–1841) and William Collins (1788–1847). Collins, for instance, achieved early fame with *The Disposal of a Favourite Lamb* (1813); it was engraved twice that year and some 15,000 of the smaller prints alone were sold.[10] It was clearly a formula that caught the popular imagination, and Collins capitalized vigorously on the fashion with subjects like *Rustic Civility* (1832),[11] showing a child holding open a gate, and its companion, *Cottage Hospitality* (1834), of a child taking broth to a poor traveller. One of his most popular pictures was *Happy as a King*:[12] the apple-cheeked children scramble on a five-barred gate, clean, dimpled, and robust despite their rags, innocent and healthy examples of the delights of rural poverty in comparison with the all too evident horrors of urban squalor which presented themselves on every side to Collins's largely urban audience.

Escapism, then, was the principal ingredient in the popularity of this genre, and it reached its ultimate expression in the work of Myles Birket Foster (1825–99). *Children Playing* (plate 26) was a large, important, and typical water-colour: carefree, pinafored children dash down a rolling hillside, pet dog scampering beside them, towards the village pond. The foreground lies in shadow, a favourite Foster device, giving the grass and undergrowth an intense blue-green which complements the hot pink-mauve tones of the girls' dresses in the heat-hazed sunlight. The land and figures are minutely worked with fine stippled touches, while the sky is delicately washed in with pale mauve graduating upwards to palest blue. Birket Foster's country people are children gambolling in nature's garden:

they gather flowers or berries, play on stiles or old logs, or, in front of cottages, listen to stories, shell peas, or tend chickens. Foster began a highly successful career as an illustrator in the 1840s, turning around 1859 to the water-colours which he continued to paint virtually without change of style for a quarter of a century. They imprinted on the English consciousness an idyllic fantasy of rural existence that was only partly countered by the social realists of the 1870s.

Foster's most popular follower was Helen Allingham (1848–1926), a water-colourist of skill and delicacy who concentrated above all on the fabric of the villages and cottages themselves, and who, in a series of exhibitions in London in the 1880s and 1890s,[13] made a practical and committed contribution to the preservationist movement then spearheaded by the Society for the Protection of Ancient Buildings, founded by William Morris in 1878. She was surprisingly impassioned, as the introduction to her 1886 exhibition catalogue (probably written by or with her husband, the poet William Allingham) revealed, and intended her drawings of Surrey cottages to be records of untouched vernacular architecture salvaged on paper as the buildings themselves were being steadily demolished at the rate of some 2,000 a year, or, almost worse, unnecessarily 'done up'. Essential modernization and sanitation were ignored while the landlord, often with a misplaced sense of duty,

> allows the agent to go round with a town architect and settle a general plan for doing up the old places (usually described as 'tumbling down' or 'falling to pieces'), a village builder makes an estimate and sends in a scratch pack of masons and joiners, and between them they often supplant fine old work, most of it firm as a rock, with poor materials and careless labour, and rub out a piece of Old England, irrecoverable henceforth by all the genius in the world and the money in the bank. . . . Whatever else is decided on, no uneven tiled roofs, with moss and houseleek, must remain, no thatch on any pretence, nor ivy on the wall, nor vine along the eaves, nor wide old chimney-places, nor roomy old staircases and cupboards. The cherry or apple-tree that pushed its blossoms almost into a lattice, will probably be cut down, and the wild rose and honeysuckle hedge be replaced by a row of pales or wires. The leaden lattice itself and all its fellows, however perfect, must inevitably give place to a set of mean little square windows of unseasoned wood – although perhaps on the very next property an architect is building imitation old cottages with lattices![14]

What this lament disregarded was the reality of the lives conducted in these picturesque cottages, and it was to this massive problem that the young social realists of the 1870s addressed themselves.

Themes of social concern had surfaced in Victorian art since the earliest years of the reign, most dramatically perhaps in the response to Thomas

Hood's *The Song of the Shirt* of 1843;[15] and increased in number with the pressure for social reform. Railways and improving communications made the countryside more accessible and so made the effects of depopulation and deprivation easier for the artist to observe. In the 1850s and 1860s Thomas Faed (1826–1900) took the example of Wilkie and produced for the Academy a series of hugely popular paintings on the theme of cottage poverty (though usually given a literary gloss with lines from Burns), while the *Illustrated London News* invented illustrated journalism and, from its first publication in 1842, printed many drawings of both urban and rural poverty. The quality of its draughtsmanship was, however, generally weak, leaving a gap in the market that was brilliantly filled in the decade from 1869 by the *Graphic*. Its drawings were powerful, the wood engraving was of the highest quality, and a great impact was made on its largely middle-class readership by a young, ambitious, and talented stable of artists who made their reputations with often raw and biting drawings, some highlighting aspects of poverty in the country which, while described in print since Cobbett, had not previously received such vivid illustration nor reached so wide an audience. Some of these artists were able to work up an Academy painting from an illustration that had been well received: the most often quoted case is that of Luke Fildes (1843–1927) whose famous documentary painting *Applicants for Admission to a Casual Ward* of 1874 (Royal Holloway College) contributed largely to the success of the first number of the *Graphic* in 1869 as a drawing called *Houseless and Hungry*.

Robert Walker Macbeth (1848–1910) was another *Graphic* artist who, though he never matched Fildes's success, painted a number of interesting East Anglian subjects. The most overtly propagandist of these was *A Lincolnshire Gang* (plate 27), shown at the Academy in 1876 with the accompanying catalogue note:

> Eight appears to be the ordinary age at which children join the agricultural gangs in the Fens; in some instances they have been known to do so even at four. It is a common practice with parents to stipulate that if the elder children are hired to the gangmaster he must take the younger ones too. The distances they have to walk, or rather run, before the labours of the day begin, are astounding; sometimes eight miles a day. They leave at five in the morning, under the care of the gangmaster, and return at five at night. They work eight or nine hours; and during the last hour they are at work, 'they will ask', said an old gangmaster, 'forty times what o'clock it is'.

The painting, now untraced, was engraved for the *Graphic*, the composition appearing in reverse: it is dawn and the exhausted women and children setting out for the fen look towards the corner of a shed where a child lies collapsed, oblivious to the menacing whip and dogs of the gangmaster, and behind them another gangmaster hauls children from a stable. It was a powerful picture, almost too powerful for the writer of the accompanying text in the *Graphic* who, like many of his contemporaries, was anxious that the subject was too painful to be used for an exhibited painting. This was a complaint often levelled at social realists throughout the reign by over-sensitive critics and by those who may have felt threatened by the potentially revolutionary use that could be made of such images.

These fears were unfounded: apart from the radical circle around William Morris, most Victorian artists were not politically involved, and the hundreds of social subject paintings that poured out in increasing quantities from the 1850s onwards[16] served as documentary and illustrative material and were not the primary social and political weapons produced by Millet and Courbet in France. Hubert Herkomer (1849–1914) was typical: the depression of the 1870s and his own somewhat self-righteously pious humanitarianism led to a decade of earnest social documentaries, like *Hard Times* (1885, Manchester), a scene of an unemployed labourer and his destitute family in a country lane. As with Frank Holl and Luke Fildes, however, the very success of the subject pictures attracted portrait commissions which rapidly took all the artists' energies and proved the making of several fortunes.

Allegory

The heightened awareness of William Blake and Samuel Palmer to the religious and mystical in nature created a visionary landscape of genius that was not matched by any Victorian artist, but outside the Pre-Raphaelite circle there were many artists whose landscapes and country figure scenes included some symbolic elements. John Linnell (1792–1882) was an intimate friend of Blake and Palmer in the early years of the century and lived on to become one of the most prosperous of the Victorian landscapists. He remained a maverick figure outside the Academy because of a dispute with Constable and, with a fierce nonconformism, painted Surrey landscapes and some biblical scenes that bore traces of the religious intensity of Blake and Palmer. *Harvest Home* (plate 28), shown at the British Institution in 1854, included some of the most potent symbols that can be found in a benevolent countryside – the harvest gathered and the day ending in a radiant sunset. These epitomized the mid-century rejection of the picturesque landscape tamed and distorted by man, and its craving for the expression of man's unity with nature. 'Of all places in the country', Linnell himself wrote,

> parks are to me the most desolate. There seems to be a dearth of intelligence and sympathy with Nature, or rather with the design of the Creator, whose thoughts or intentions are not perceived because men

> seek to bend Nature to express their sense of their own importance, their riches and powers; and they put Nature as far as they can into a kind of livery, as they do their servants, degrading both with what pretends to be ornament. The landscape is reduced to a toy-shop sentiment on a large scale; everything is denuded of those accompaniments which give the true expression of grandeur or beauty to the scene.
>
> It is true the trees are left to grow unrestrained, looking like aristocratic 'swells', isolated from all the undergrowth; and, with the ground shaved under them, they look like large toy-trees placed upon a green board. It is not until one gets upon a common, near a forest, or into farmlands, that one begins to breathe again, and feel out of the influence of man's despotism. Man stamps his own thought and character upon everything he meddles with, and, unhappily in most cases, he obliterates the work of God and substitutes his own.[17]

Linnell, however, was prepared to exploit man's ingenuity when it suited him; like many other mid-century artists from the Pre-Raphaelites to Courbet, he is known to have used photographs, and Aaron Scharf suggests that some of Linnell's seething skies and rustic scenes may even have been taken from photographs not of English but of Italian landscape.[18]

The desire to represent God's work in nature at its most unremitting was a sentiment thoroughly understood by Peter Graham (1836–1921), one of a large group of Edinburgh-trained Scottish artists including Orchardson, MacWhirter, and Pettie who came south to conquer the Academy in the 1860s. Graham succeeded beyond his wildest hopes with his first Academy picture, *A Spate in the Highlands* of 1866 (plate 29). Its impressive cataract of water and swirling mists recalled something of Turner's effects, but made specific with the tiny figure of a herdsman driving his animals back from the broken bridge, the brink of the abyss, so that *The Times*'s reviewer felt moved to speak of the subject's 'soul-subduing' impact.[19] Graham strove for an expression of the sublime terror which could confront man in the face of nature; G. J. Pinwell (1842–75), one of the brilliant young illustrators who revived black and white wood engraving in the 1860s, had a gift for farmyard and village scenes that bear a curiously claustrophobic weight of foreboding. One of Pinwell's most overtly symbolic drawings was *The Shadow* (plate 30):[20] children drag a calf to slaughter while the farmer stands framed by a grisly gibbet of predatory birds, the final manifestations of man's bloody exploitation of nature.

Pinwell was a member of the circle around George Heming Mason (1818–72) and Fred Walker (1840–75) who between them created in the late 1860s and 1870s what many critics called the first new school in English art since the Pre-Raphaelites. They were eclectic, wildly so to modern eyes, and ranged easily from the modern French realists like Millet and

Jules Breton (though eschewing radical politics) to the early Renaissance and classical sculpture. In *The Plough* (Tate) of 1870, Walker placed a ploughing team, drawn from a group of a boy and horses in the Elgin Marbles, against a stratified, mannered landscape which, though taken from a Somerset quarry, has the air of a Bellini background; Walker had prepared himself for the painting by reading Thomson's *The Seasons* and Bloomfield's *The Farmer's Boy*.[21] The curiously still, frieze-like result was far removed from the muscular immediacy of *An English Ploughing Match* (plate 31) by William Small (1843–1931), engraved for the *Graphic* in 1875. There is sweat on the horses' rumps, the ploughmen are heroic labourers, and the earth curls and crumbles under the onslaught of the blades. It was a dynamic image that anticipated the socialist realism of this century and made Walker's *Plough* seem an effete archaism.

During the same decade, Sir Coutts Lindsay opened the Grosvenor Gallery, his show place for such aesthetic refugees from the Academy as Burne-Jones, Whistler, Tissot, and Watts. The first Grosvenor exhibition of 1877 included *The Reaper and the Flowers* (plate 32) by Philip Richard Morris (1836–1902). It is an odd picture, absolutely English in its sentimental and naïve symbolism, and part of a certain absolutely consistent English idea of the rural idyll. It was hardly surprising, therefore, that those artists who had seen the revolution effected by impressionism in France should have reacted so violently against such a literary view of nature and such an anecdotal kind of symbolism. The New English Art Club, founded in 1886, brought together those young artists like Steer, Sickert, and Clausen who in varying ways had found new approaches in France to the whole concept of what a picture should be. George Clausen (1852–1944) was an interestingly transitional figure who, though sophisticated enough to look to France, was led by an inescapably Victorian sentiment to take as his master not Monet or Pissarro, but Millet's academic follower, Jules Bastien-Lepage. Bastien-Lepage was a dogmatic *plein air* painter: that is, as far as possible the whole of his often busy canvases had to be painted on site and in consistent light which, as he worked in northern France, gave his pictures their characteristic grey tonality. Clausen, in an essay published in 1892,[22] wrote of Bastien's simple acceptance of nature that allowed him to balance the literary and the purely aesthetic elements in his art and supported his purist rejection of studio painting. Clausen also recognized that Bastien took care to choose 'a good type'[23] in his pictures of peasants working on the land – a practice that was thoroughly in sympathy with the Victorian interest in 'types' from Dickens onwards. *The Stone Pickers* of 1887 (plate 33) shows how well Clausen learned. It is painted with his square brush stroke and restricted, near-monochrome palette, its sombre greys and browns sharpened with acidic green grass out of which the daisies and cornflowers struggle in frail contrast to the pile of jagged grey stones in the foreground. Clausen had made of the girl a grey, ghostly symbol of rural poverty, using the language of the end of the century, but still in an essentially Victorian state of mind.

The 1890s found artists of every persuasion still looking to nature and finding in it the most diverse inspirations. Philip Wilson Steer painted the light and sparkling coast at Walberswick in the spirit of Monet and Renoir; Arnesby Brown and Henry William Banks Davis produced cattle in sun-dappled meadows and fording Welsh rivers with a full range of well-learnt impressionist technique. Arthur Hacker plumbed the depths of silliness with airbrushed nudes in sylvan glades and drifts of leaves; and Robert Bevan painted Exmoor in the spirit of Gauguin. The reign had begun with Ruskin's exhortation to artists to represent nature 'in all singleness of heart';[24] it ended in the decade of Picasso and Braque. In over sixty years, Victorian artists had given their audience many vivid evocations of both a generalized nature and of specific locations, and had also explored social and philosophical issues as they affected rural life. England had not produced a Millet or a Courbet, but the profound nostalgia of the urban middle classes for their rural past ensured the survival, in however changed a form, of the English landscape in art.

Notes

1 Hardie, 1968, III.
2 See Parris, 1973, for a comprehensive survey.
3 Rosenblum, 1961, 350–9.
4 The title continues: 'their superiority in the art of landscape painting to all the ancient masters proved by examples of the True, the Beautiful, and the Intellectual, from the works of modern artists, especially from those of J. M. W. Turner, Esq., R.A.'.
5 Staley, 1973, 185.
6 Cooper, 1890, I, 183.
7 Forbes, 1975, 88.
8 In the collection of Lord Hollenden until 1958, now untraced and represented here by the reduced replica of 1897.
9 Lusk, 1901, 6.
10 'Pictures and Stories', *Connoisseur*, April 1957, CXXXIX, 147.
11 Original picture exhibited at the Royal Academy in 1832; version dated 1833, Sheepshanks Collection, Victoria and Albert Museum, London.
12 The original of this was shown at the Academy in 1836, but was best known from the engraving of 1839 and the replica painted for the collector Robert Vernon, presented with the rest of his major collection of contemporary art to the nation in 1847 and now in the Tate Gallery, London.
13 The Fine Art Society, London, exhibition nos. 41, 1886; 66, 1889; 118, 1894.
14 'A Collection of Drawings by Mrs Allingham, RWS, illustrating Surrey Cottages', The Fine Art Society, London, prefatory note, p. 4.
15 *Great Victorian Pictures*, 1978, 71.
16 Rodee, 1977, 307–13.
17 Story, 1892, II, 50–1.
18 Scharf, 1974, 115.

19 *Great Victorian Pictures*, 1978, 41.
20 Engraved by the Brothers Dalziel for Robert Buchanan (ed.), *Wayside Posies: Original Poems of the Country Life*, Routledge, London, 1867, p. 1.
21 Marks, 1896, 192–3.
22 Theuriet, 1892, 111–27.
23 ibid., 117.
24 Cook and Wedderburn, 1903, III, 624.

22 John Constable, *Arundel Mill and Castle*, 1837. Oil on canvas; 28½ × 39½ in., 72·4 × 100·3 cm (The Toledo Museum of Art, Toledo, Ohio).

23 J. M. W. Turner, *Norham Castle, Sunrise*, *c.* 1835–40. Oil on canvas; $35\frac{3}{4} \times 48$ in. 91×122 cm (By kind permission of the Tate Gallery, London)

24 Frederick Richard Lee and Thomas Sidney Cooper, *The Chequered Shade*, 1854. Oil on canvas; 78 × 66 in., 198·1 × 167·6 cm (The Forbes Magazine Collection, New York).

25 Benjamin Williams Leader, *At evening time it shall be light*, 1897. Oil on canvas; $30\frac{1}{8} \times 50\frac{1}{8}$ in., $76{\cdot}5 \times 127{\cdot}3$ cm (By kind permission of the

26 Myles Birket Foster, *Children Playing*, 1886. Watercolour; 13¼ × 27⅝ in., 33·7 × 70·2 cm (By kind permission of the Victoria and Albert Museum, London).

27 Robert Walker Macbeth, *A Lincolnshire Gang*. Wood engraving, after the untraced oil painting, publ. *Graphic*, vol. 14, 60–1, 15 July 1876 (The Witt Library, Courtauld Institute of Art).

28 John Linnell, *Harvest Home, Sunset: The Last Road*, 1853, exh. 1854. Oil on canvas; $34\frac{3}{4} \times 58$ in., $88{\cdot}3 \times 147{\cdot}3$ cm (By kind permission of the Tate Gallery, London).

29 Peter Graham, *A Spate in the Highlands*, 1866. Oil on canvas; 47¼ × 69⅝ in., 120 × 176·8 cm (By kind permission of the Manchester City Art

30 George John Pinwell, *The Shadow*, 1867. Wood engraving; 6⅝ × 4⅞ in., 16·9 × 12·5 cm (The Witt Library, Courtauld Institute of Art).

31 William Small, *An English Ploughing Match*, 1875. Wood engraving; 12¾ × 18½ in., 35 × 47 cm (publ. *Graphic*, vol. 11, between pages 264 and 265

32 Philip Richard Morris, *The Reaper and the Flowers*, 1877. Oil on canvas; 35 × 59 in., 88·9 × 149·9 cm (Ex collection Captain Henry Hill) (engraved by Charles Roberts, repr. *Magazine of Art*, 1902, p. 423. The Witt Library, Courtauld Institute of Art).

33 George Clausen, *The Stone Pickers*, 1887. Oil on canvas; 51 × 30 in., 129·5 × 76·2 cm (Laing Gallery, Newcastle-upon-Tyne. The Witt Library, Courtauld Institute of Art).

5

Landscape in nineteenth-century literature

Louis James

A landscape in literature is a view, not only of countryside, but of the moral and social attitudes of writer and reader. In the nineteenth century the upheavals in the intellectual background revealed themselves in attitudes to nature, and in the way nature was portrayed. This was complicated by other developments – geological studies; discoveries by the Pre-Raphaelite painters about the appearance of light and shadow; the popularity from the 1850s of photography, and the changing face of the Victorian countryside itself. But here also one is dealing with ideas. The discovery even of photography led to debates as to how the new medium should be used to select and interpret nature; as P. H. Emerson urged. '[The photographer] must learn, as the painter has to do, to distinguish what in nature is really suitable for pictorial purposes.'[1]

Jane Austen (1775–1817) is a transitional writer. Living an uneventful life in a narrow provincial society, she may seem an unlikely choice as a landscape writer. Yet her concern with the moral development of her characters in a precisely charted social milieu gave a sharp edge to the way the country reflected the moral attitudes of those who inhabited it. In *Northanger Abbey* (written from 1798, published in 1818), 'natural' views of the countryside are complicated by the concepts of the 'picturesque' popularized in particular by William Gilpin (1724–1804), author of a series of illustrated tours including *The Wye and South Wales* (1782) and *The Lakes* (1789). Gilpin described the 'picturesque' as 'that kind of beauty which would look well in a picture', and developed the eighteenth-century practice of selecting from the multiplicity of nature its 'ideal' and most perfect forms with his prescription of 'high-colouring' heightening the romantic effect.[2] The heroine of Austen's novel, Catherine Morland, is enthralled to discover that, by precepts of the picturesque, 'it seemed as if a good view were no longer to be taken from the top of an high hill, and that a clear blue sky was no longer the proof of a fine day. She was heartily ashamed of her ignorance' – and confronted with a good view, 'she voluntarily rejected the whole city of Bath, as unworthy to make part of a landscape'.[3]

Jane Austen rejected the excesses of the 'picturesque', but this does not mean that she admired landscape as untouched nature. *Pride and Prejudice* (begun in 1796, published in 1831), for instance, concerns the misunderstandings and final reconciliation between the vivacious Elizabeth Bennet and reserved, socially poised Fitzwilliam Darcy. After a letter has shown Elizabeth that she has damagingly misjudged Darcy, she goes north to visit his estate, Pemberley. The landscape may, on first reading, appear natural.

> they pursued the accustomed circuit, which brought them again, after some time, in a descent among hanging woods, to the edge of the water, in one of its narrowest parts. They crossed it by a simple bridge in character with the general air of the scene; it was a spot less adorned than any they had yet visited; and the valley, here contracted into a glen, allowed room only for the stream, and a narrow walk amidst the rough coppice-wood which bordered it. Elizabeth longed to explore its windings.[4]

The scene, however, is perfectly 'picturesque' – natural, but with its natural beauty gently accentuated – the valley crowding into the glen, the contrast between the snaking stream and the rough coppice woods. In particular, the man-made objects are those which perfectly reflect the natural – the bridge is 'simple', in character with the general air of the scene; the walk is narrow to fit in with the glen. Gilpin specified that as nature should have the heightened order of art, so art – including houses, bridges, and paths – should reflect the harmony of nature. The scene also has a deeper purpose. Darcy, like Pemberton, balances natural impulse with the orders and restraints of civilization. Observing the estate and the hall – which shows similar qualities – Elizabeth understands his moral character, and is drawn further towards accepting him.

The use of landscape to reflect moral character goes back to the origins of the novel. In Fielding's *Tom Jones* (1749), for instance, Squire Allworthy, who, as magistrate, mediates God's wisdom to his community,[5] is introduced in the context of Allworthy Hall, Gothic in its profusion, Grecian in its balance, and built to perfectly harmonize with hill, valley, and lake.[6] By the end of the eighteenth century, however, the social upheavals of the French Revolution, war in Europe, and the intensifying effects of enclosure and rural poverty at home, were all disintegrating the social image of the estate as an ideal. Jane Austen's *Mansfield Park* (begun in 1812, published in 1814) reflects both disturbance and nostalgia. The order of the park which gives the book its name is being undermined both within and without. The new generation lack the social values embodied in the stern but good-hearted Sir Thomas Bertram; while he is away even the physical order of the house is disrupted and a stage for amateur theatricals is built outside his study. In wider society at the time the debate continued between Edmund Burke's *Reflections on the French Revolution* (1790), defending gradual social change, and Thomas Paine's defence of *The French Revolution* (1791). In *Mansfield Park* the beauty of the English estates that have gradually evolved from Elizabethan times are being wantonly destroyed by the morally shallow characters such as Mr Rushwood, Henry Crawford, and even the minor character, Mrs Norris.[7] By contrast the lower-class girl who is adopted into the family and is to emerge as the heroine, Fanny Price, protests against the 'improvers', and Edmund, who is to marry her, puts an argument against rash changes in a form that might have been phrased by Burke. 'I should not put myself into the hands of an improver. I would rather have an inferior degree of beauty, of my own choice and acquired gradually.'[8]

The book also reflects other changes in the attitude to landscape. Compare the experience of Elizabeth Bennet contemplating Pemberley, with that of Fanny sitting in a formal garden:

> [They] sauntered about together many an half hour in Mrs Grant's shrubbery, the weather being unusually mild for the time of year; and venturing even to sit down on one of the benches now comparatively unsheltered, remaining there perhaps till in the midst of some tender ejaculation of Fanny's, on the sweets of so protracted an autumn, they were forced by the sudden swell of a cold gust shaking down the last few yellow leaves about them, to jump up and walk for warmth.[9]

It is important that it is the lower-middle-class Fanny who is at the centre of the experience: it is not filtered through an inherited cultural awareness. Yet it also reflects a shift in the wider focus of the novel. The objective order of the landscape is retreating; the reader is becoming more directly involved in the subjective awareness of the characters, the senses, atmosphere, the personal reaction to exterior reality.

This shift in consciousness of the countryside can be associated with the romantic movement. This movement is so complex and so well known that it is impossible to say anything incisive about it in a brief compass. Yet as it overshadowed Victorian attitudes to nature – even when in reaction to it – it is equally impossible to ignore. One can do worse than begin with one of Wordsworth's most familiar poems, 'Lines Composed a Few Miles above Tintern Abbey . . . July 13, 1798'. The subject is not a new one – the Wye Valley appeared briefly in Pope's 'Epistle to Bathurst' (1733) as the setting for John Kyrle's benevolent estate, and its beauties were intimately described in one of Gilpin's tours.[10] Wordsworth's word picture inherits much eighteenth-century diction, and to some extent the compositional eye of the picturesque.

> The day is come when I again repose
> Here, under this dark sycamore, and view
> These plots of cottage-ground, these orchard-tufts
> Which, at this season with their unripe fruits,
> Are clad in one green hue, and lose themselves
> 'Mid groves and copses. Once again I see
> These hedge-rows, hardly hedge-rows, little lines
> Of sportive wood run wild: these pastoral farms,
> Green to the very door; and wreathes of smoke
> Sent up, in silence, from among the trees! (ll. 9–18)

One notices first the date of the poem, thought important enough to be included in the title: the piece was composed mentally by Wordsworth while sitting on the hillside, although it was written down some days later. Like Coleridge's 'Frost at Midnight', written five months earlier to record sitting by the fire on a still winter's night, the lines are about a precise and unique moment. The eighteenth-century view of landscape was concerned with the ideal, the generalized, and the timeless. Penetrating beneath the poetic terms – groves, sportive woods, pastoral farms – one finds a sense of exact detail: the apples grown but still green in mid-July; the grass growing over the thresholds of the lonely cottages; the hesitation, encapsulated in the lines, as how precisely to describe the untrimmed hedgerows, and the moment of movement in stillness in the image of the silent, rising smoke. The scene is also interfused with its meaning for the viewer. Landscape becomes more than a giver of heightened sensations: it is an active element working on the individual, a 'medicine' for the soul suffering from the effects of weariness, doubt, and the pressures of an increasingly urbanized society. As 'Lines . . . above Tintern Abbey' continued,

> But oft, in lonely rooms, and 'mid the din
> Of towns and cities, I have owed to them
> In hours of weariness, sensations sweet,
> Felt in the blood, and felt along the heart;
> And passing even into my purer mind,
> With tranquil restoration:– (ll. 25–31)

The experiences Wordsworth is responding to here are those already implanted in childhood, and however much he appealed to Victorian adult nostalgia for the country, his verse essentially linked nature to the child. Although in later life he was anxious to avoid implications of pantheism, his experience of nature was, in a direct way, religious; the soul nurtured in the countryside is in touch with 'the essential passions of the heart',[11] the 'sacred simplicities of life'.[12] In analysing his own experience, Wordsworth recorded that the restorative powers of nature brought both the power of feeling and a mystical sense freed from the confines of dogma.

It was in these terms that he had perhaps his most dramatic impact on Victorian intellectuals. John Stuart Mill records in his autobiography how he suffered a form of mental breakdown as the result of the intensive education to which his father had subjected him from the age of 3, when he began to learn Greek. At the age of 20, in 1826, he read Wordsworth's *Lyrical Ballads*. As he noted,

> What made Wordsworth's poems a medicine for my state of mind, was that they expressed, not mere outward beauty, but states of feeling, and of thought coloured by feeling, under the excitement of beauty. They seemed to be the very culture of the feeling, which I was in quest of.[13]

'Mark Rutherford' (Hale White) had a similar recovery, not from the rigours of utilitarian philosophy and the classics, but from a narrow, nonconformist belief. For him, reading the *Lyrical Ballads*

> excited a movement and a growth that went on till, by degrees, all the systems which enveloped me like a body gradually decayed from me and fell away into nothing. . . . Wordsworth unconsciously did for me what every religious reformer has done – he re-created my Supreme Divinity substituting a new and living spirit for the old deity, once alive, but gradually hardened into an idol.[14]

Later in the smoke and crowds of London, he found himself strengthened by his 'early training on the "Lyrical Ballads" '.[15]

For the mass of Wordsworth's readers, however, he was associated not so much with philosophy and religion as with the Lake District. When his house at Rydal Mount became an object for pilgrimage, Matthew Arnold recorded in 1879, 'I remember Wordsworth relating how one of the pilgrims, a clergyman, asked him if he had ever written anything besides the *Guide to the Lakes*. Yes, he answered modestly, he had written verses.'[16] The specific regionalism of English country literature was one of its features as the century progressed. The most extensive rural poem before Wordsworth's *Prelude* (completed in 1805, published in 1850) was *The Seasons* (1726–30) by James Thomson (1700–46). Thomson covers the whole spectrum of eighteenth-century attitudes to nature, from the tropics to the Arctic, from the theological to the scientific.

Robert Bloomfield was drawn to poetry largely by the example of Thomson. Starting life as a plough boy at Honington near Bury, he came to London in 1781 and worked as a shoemaker. Making verses in his head as he worked, amid the bustle of the workshop, he composed *The Farmer's*

Boy (1800), describing the rural year. In under three years it reputedly sold 26,000 copies. He was praised for writing descriptions 'not like the Poem of Thomson, taking a wide excursion through all the phaenomena of the *Seasons*, but nearly limited to the rural *occupation* and business of the fields, the dairy and the farm yard'.[17] Today the fresh observation of farm life, unsustained by much original talent, does not survive the heavy poetic diction, or Bloomfield's determination to compose his memories into 'pretty' scenes for his readers. But the concern with the actual, not the general, was a new element, reinforced by the detailed woodcut vignettes that accompanied it. The new developments in etching across the grain of boxwood, pioneered by Thomas Bewick (1753–1828), itself brought a new precise awareness of the detail of country scenery, birds, and animals to a wide range of readers.

John Clare (1793–1864) at one time a herd-boy, and later a small farmer, had a much greater talent than Bloomfield, both of observation and of the use of language. His *Shepherd's Calendar* (1827) also inevitably echoes Thomson, but one is not simply in an actual countryside, the details are precise, sometimes overloaded:

> Blackening through the evening sky
> In clouds the starnels daily fly
> To Whittlesea's reed-wooded mere,
> And osier holts by rivers near.[18]

Bloomfield's accounts of the farmer's experience – pleasure, fatigue, cold – are poetically distanced. Clare conveys as from within the often exhausting interaction of man, land, and nature:

> The ploughmen maul along the doughy sloughs
> And often stop their songs, to clean their ploughs
> From teasing twitch, that in the spongy soil
> Clings round the coulter, interrupting toil . . .
> While far above, the solitary crane
> Swings lonely to unfrozen dykes again,
> Cranking a jarring melancholy cry
> Through the wild journey of the cheerless sky.[19]

The scene is experienced through the body of the ploughman. Clare's strength, and his weakness, was his speed of composition: he catches a moment in all its detail, producing a phrase of brilliant clarity, but may then lapse into the banal. But his collected work gives a wide-ranging picture of the nature and life of Northamptonshire in the early nineteenth century. From 1835 social and emotional pressures became too intense for him. He was confined as insane, and the nature he had observed objectively became, in a few extraordinary poems, experienced from within. In 'Clock-a-Clay', for example, he actually becomes a ladybird sheltering in a cowslip during a storm:

> While grassy forest quakes surprise,
> And the wild wind sobs and sighs,
> My gold home rocks as like to fall
> On its pillars green and tall;
> When the pattering rain drives by
> Clock-a-clay keeps warm and dry.[20]

Further south in Dorset, William Barnes (1801–86), a country schoolmaster and later parson, combined an empathy with the countryside with a very different temperament. While Clare's insights are intense and luminous, Barnes's lyrical verse is low-keyed, in touch with slower rhythms of everyday farming life. In his poems the art is almost invisible – that is its art.

> Well, today then I shall roll off on the road
> Round by Woodcombe, out to Shellbrook, to the mill,
> With my brand-new little spring-cart, with a load,
> To come loadless round by Chalk-hill, at my will:
> As the whole day will be dry,
> By the token of the sky,
> Come to meet me, with the children on the road.[21]

His search for ways to express country life led him to experiment with a dialect to which he was native, although as a schoolmaster he would normally speak standard English. Clare's poetry also often made use of local words.[22] Dialects were an important element in the rural tradition, and did penetrate sporadically into written literature through works such as John Collier's *A View of the Lancashire Dialect*, published as early as 1746, but reprinted and imitated well into the nineteenth century. Tennyson also wrote verse in his native Lincolnshire dialect,[23] and his reading – still preserved on an early phonograph recording – indicates how the rhythms and tones of this lie behind even his verse in standard English. In the poetry of Barnes, consider how the lyrical flow of the above passage is strengthened in the dialect version:

> Well, to-day Jeänne is my set time to goo
> To the grist-mill out at Sherbrook under Bere,
> Wi' my spring-cart out in cart house, vier new,
> An' zome grist corn, to come womeward wi' en leer.
> Zoo's the whole day will be dry,
> By the readership of the sky,
> Come to meet me, wi' the children, on the road.[24]

Barnes's verse had a select but discriminating audience in the Victorian period, including Tennyson, the Brownings, and Coventry Patmore. But it was in his influence on and relationship to Thomas Hardy that he made his most important impact. Barnes illustrated for Hardy not only the resources of dialect, the inter-relationship of scenery and people, but a sense of the rhythms of country life, of attitudes to experience that were different from those of educated town folk. A central theme in Hardy's work is the conflict between the accepting country culture and intellectual sensibility – Eustacia Vye, Tess, Jude. Barnes gave a voice to the continuing culture of the Dorset folk from which these figures were tragically alienated.

Awareness of the rural condition, however, also brought a sense of the suffering and disruption of rural life. By the fourth edition of Clare's *Poems Descriptive* (1820), 'Helpstone' was docked of ten lines attacking the exploitation of the labourers – 'Accursed Wealth, o'erbounding human laws'. His poem 'The Village Funeral' breaks off its description in anger against the effects of the Poor Laws and the general indifference to the 'fatherless' who 'stroll in their rags unnoticed through the street'. 'Helpstone Green' records how both the human and physical life of the village were being affected by the enclosures

> Both milkmaid's shouts and herdman's call
>   Have vanish'd with the green,
> The kingcups yellow, shades and all,
>   Shall never more be seen;
> But the thick-cultur'd tribes that grow
>   Will so efface the scene,
> That after-times will hardly know
>   It ever was a green.[25]

Barnes, too, was drawn into Dorset rural life by his concern with the rural suffering that he saw, and wrote six eclogues, including 'The Commons A-Took in' and 'The Unioners', which explored the effects of enclosure, the Poor Laws, and rural depopulation.

For social protest against rural conditions, however, one turns to the tradition begun by George Crabbe (1754–1832) whose poem *The Village* (1783) was an angry rebuttal to Oliver Goldsmith's sentimentalized picture of rural decay, *The Deserted Village* (1770). In the ninenteenth century Crabbe published further volumes concerned with country and small-town life in the area of his native Aldeburgh in Suffolk – *The Parish Registry* (1807), *The Borough* (1810), *Tales* (1812), and *Tales of the Hall* (1819). His stories make up a sharply realistic spectrum of country society. He is concerned with landscape in a neutral way; not as a world of beauty, but a grey fen countryside dominated by mudflats, waterweeds, docks, and mallow, which stands as an unemphasized background to the often grim life of his characters.

Ebenezer Elliott (1781–1849), a Sheffield master-founder and poet, was best known for his *Corn-Law Rhymes* (1828), which dramatized the plight of the poor who were unable to afford tax-protected bread. In his sympathies he can be seen primarily as a northern town dweller. Yet, his concern with city life was inseparable from his rural interests. Here he strongly rejected any association with Wordsworth, whom he saw as describing the sufferings of the poor without protesting against the social injustices that caused them, and claimed Crabbe as his model. In *The Village Patriarch* (1829) he uses his image of an old man, Enoch Wray, returned from abroad and revisiting the countryside of his childhood. It is now built over by industry:

> New streets invade the country, and he strays,
> Lost in strange paths, still seeking, and in vain
> For ancient landmarks[26]

As he explores the countryside, he finds there the enclosures denying the peasant his traditional livelihood, and even the rural industries such as the water mill are ruined and derelict before the competition of steam. In this context nature itself turns malevolent, like the weeds clogging the millwheel and the otter and water rat chasing the trout through the miller's sunken boat.

> What is this plague, unsearchable and lone,
> Sightless and tongueless, till a wild voice howls
> When nations die?[27]

Like William Morris in *News from Nowhere* (1891) towards the end of the century, Elliott can only look forward to an apocalyptic age in which the forces of industry, 'though their iron roots seem fast', will also pass and the balance of man with nature be recovered.

Clare, Barnes, Crabbe, and Elliott are all distinctively linked to the regions in which they wrote. Indeed, a major feature of literature of the country throughout the nineteenth century is the development of a sense of the difference between the English regions. George Eliot becomes associated with the Warwickshire Midlands; the Brontës with the Yorkshire countryside around Haworth; Tennyson constantly returns to the Lincolnshire wolds; Mrs Gaskell comes to be seen as a Manchester writer; Hardy creates Wessex out of the Dorset region. Particularly in the north, the development, with the industrial revolution, of new urban communities created intellectual circles with writers anxious to explore the resources of their local landscape: Robert Story and James Armstrong wrote of Northumbria, John Nicholson of the Airedale Valley, William Heaton published *Flowers of Calderdale* (1844), and a collection such as William Andrews's *North Country Poets* (1888) points to other similar examples.[28]

Where writers were not associated with one area they characteristically spent time detailing specific locales. As Myron Brightfield notes in his monumental compilation, *Victorian England in its Novels, 1840–1870* (1968),

> terrain, altitude, and other geophysical influences were sufficient to produce the individual differences which characterized the landscape of various districts of the island. The Englishman who knew his own country was able to recognize, within almost every county, the distinctively local manifestations of natural beauty.[29]

As communications, particularly railways, made provincial areas of the country more accessible, and as improving standards of living afforded a larger number of people leisure to explore, the Victorian reader became increasingly interested in regional characteristics. By mid-century the guidebook and postcard view industries were beginning to develop.[30] Thus literature used regional locations to give sharper definition, and at the same time country areas were of interest because of their literary associations: pilgrims would visit Rydal Mount to see Wordsworth; Reading and nearby Three Mile Cross were known as the setting for Mary Mitford's stories; Mrs Gaskell's researches around Haworth, recounted in her life of Charlotte Brontë,[31] encouraged visits to the Brontë country.

In 1847 the railway opened up the Lake District to the northern cities. As already noted, many who used it knew Wordsworth's *Guide* better than his poetry, and by the mid-Victorian age the romantic interest in nature as a spiritual force had given way before more secular views. Matthew Arnold, who himself had grown up in the Lake District under the friendly eye of Wordsworth, loved the area, but rejected its spiritual influence on the child.[32] John Ruskin had an even more ambivalent attitude to romantic views. He held a profoundly religious attitude to nature, and his life's work was a constantly extending exploration of what he saw as the interconnected web of God's creation. Yet he was profoundly mistrustful of Wordsworth's tendencies to elevate created nature itself into an object of worship. For Ruskin one must begin, not with spiritual or emotional experience, but with a strictly disciplined exploration of 'the inexhaustible perfection of nature's details'. In a famous passage he called on the artist to 'go to Nature in all singleness of heart . . . rejecting nothing, selecting nothing, and scorning nothing, believing all things are right and good, and rejoicing always in the truth'.[33]

Equally well known is the work of the diverse group of artists whom Ruskin was to champion, and who in 1848 formed themselves into the Pre-Raphaelite Brotherhood. They were also opposed to the numinous, attempting an exhaustive accuracy to the reality that they saw. They took painting out of the studio to the precise locality, even though for Holman Hunt when working on *The Scapegoat* this meant a perilous journey to the Dead Sea, and in order for him to catch a specific effect of dawn for *The Light of the World* he had to wait up night after night in a shelter composed of hay bales. The Pre-Raphaelites spent months on the detail of grasses and foliage. They discovered new qualities of colour, light, and shade. Through their work, and through their impact on Victorian art and literature, they reinforced a concern with the specific, the regional. So, Ford Madox Brown recorded in *An English Autumn Afternoon* still-rural Hampstead in the 1850s; and Holman Hunt's *Hireling Shepherd* details the scenery on the banks of the Ewell river.

Yet, from the variety of Pre-Raphaelite landscape painting, a particular image of the countryside emerges. It is of a still moment, usually in summer or autumn, heavy with sensations. It is the landscape of Ford Madox Brown's *Pretty Baa Lambs*, John Everett Millais' *The Blind Girl*, Arthur Hughes's *Home from the Sea* or John Brett's *The Stone-breaker*. Nor is this exclusive to painting. To take a few examples at random, it is there in the novel, in the glowing landscapes of George Eliot's *Mill on the Floss* or David's first experiences of Blunderstone in *David Copperfield*; in poems such as Matthew Arnold's *Scholar Gipsy* (1853) and George Meredith's *Love in the Valley* (1851); or in D. G. Rossetti's sonnet 'Silent Noon' (1881):

> The pasture gleams and glooms
> 'Neath billowing skies that scatter and amass.
> All round our nest, far as the eye can pass,
> Are golden kingcup-fields with silver edge
> Where the cow-parsley skirts the hawthorn-hedge.
> 'Tis visible silence, still as the hour-glass.
> Deep in the sun-searched growths the dragon-fly
> Hangs like a blue thread loosened from the sky:
> So, this winged hour is dropped to us from above.

It is a sense of countryside where everything is fertile, secure, small in scale, overlaid with associations. It is recognizably 'English'.

It is relevant to point out, as Raymond Williams does in *The Country and the City*,[34] that it is not necessarily 'England', and that, until Hardy, Victorian novelists of the country were largely out of touch with the realities of rural life. But it is also true that writers were often aware of what they were doing when they portrayed idyllic country scenes. These are often associated with childhood, making the point that, as with Maggie Tulliver or David Copperfield, adult experience will destroy this Eden. Where rural life is asserted as an ideal, as at the end of George Eliot's *Silas Marner*, acceptance of the quiet country life reflects acceptance of Victorian moral values. As George Levine has noted, the Victorian image of the countryside is contrasted with that of mountain or desert. Mountains reflect disquiet, questing, the unreality found by the Dorrit family in

Dickens's novel when they visit the Alps. The gentle fields and woods of England image security, balance – a world known and accepted. 'Victorian fiction' (and, one might add, poetry) 'typically lives at low altitudes. . . . Victorian novelists . . . tended to place happiness in bounded human landscapes.'[35]

Under the pressure of materialism and city life, Victorian writers turned to the past or the future to find rural settings. George Eliot characteristically wrote of the earlier years of the century.[36] Matthew Arnold, caught in 'this strange disease of modern life,/With its sick hurry, its divided aims',[37] recreated in *The Scholar Gipsy* the seventeenth-century Oxford world when an undergraduate could lose himself in rural life. The Victorian quest for the Gothic and the medieval was, among other things, the search for a preindustrial world in which nature was unspolit. Thus Thomas Carlyle's *Past and Present* (1843) contrasts Victorian society with that of the twelfth century, when 'the Ribble and the Aire roll down, as yet unpolluted by dyer's chemistry; tenanted by merry trout and piscatory otters; the sunbeam and the vacant wind's blast alone traversing these moors'. William Morris's *News from Nowhere* (1891), a dream of autumn of travelling up the Thames in the twenty-first century, when revolution has abolished capitalist industry, can be read as escapism. Certainly the sun shines continuously. But Morris's rural paradise is constructed throughout from his socialist theory, down to the open countryside which has reasserted itself with the ending of enclosure and capitalist farming. It ends with a rediscovery of his own house near Oxford, whose rural peace has been a foretaste of the possible future.

Yet even Morris's ideal world contains doubts – inhabitants unhappy with the new world, unanswered questions about political organizations, human motivation, age, and disease. The countryside portrayed by the Pre-Raphaelites, too, rarely could rest in the simple acceptance of nature. Stephens had recommended: 'Believe that there is that in the fact of truth, though it is only in the character of a leaf earnestly studied, which may do its share in the great labours of the world.'[38] Yet their painting characteristically moves away from total objectivity towards moral meanings – telling a story, emblematic details, or, with artists like D. G. Rossetti or Burne-Jones, mystical and symbolic reality. From their first days the Brotherhood debated the nature that they were trying to portray – was it the actual world, or a reflex in the mind of this reality, recreated through art?[39]

A number of their paintings were based on poems by Alfred Lord Tennyson, and his work reflects the same debate. His early poem, *The Palace of Art* (1832), is concerned with the morality of imaginative worlds themselves. It describes the artist who created a pleasure house of art, only to find that it atrophied and was in need of purgation before it could return to the 'reality' of the world. At the end of the poem, however, the palace is left standing. *The Lady of Shallott* (1832) is even more ambivalent. The story is well known. The lady is doomed to sit in her tower, seeing the countryside only in the reflex in her mirror, weaving this into a 'magic web'. She is 'half sick of shadows', and the beauty of Sir Lancelot draws her to look at him directly: as she dies her body is borne down the river to Camelot and the life she has been denied.

One meaning of the poem is reasonably clear: the lady is like the artist in weaving art from his image of reality. But what are the conclusions? If the artist sees reality as 'shadows', can he do anything else? What is the only reality he can know? In *Mariana* (1830), illustrated by Millais, Tennyson portrayed a moment of stillness and heat close to that characteristic of Pre-Raphaelite painting, which has now become a burden. 'She wept, "I am aweary, aweary,/O God that I were dead." ' The poem looks forward to D. G. Rossetti's *The Orchard Pit* (1886) where, in a more symbolic image, the spirit of autumn and fruition is linked with that of decay and death.

Questions about the reality of nature were implied in wider questions about the meaning of created nature. A series of works, including Charles Lyell's *Principles of Geology* (1830–3), Robert Chambers's *Vestiges of Creation* (1844), and later, Charles Darwin's *The Origin of Species* (1859), questioned the biblical account of creation and the centrality of man in nature.[40] Tennyson's *In Memoriam* (1850) was a series of short poems forming a diary of his grief for his intimate friend Arthur Hallam, who died in Vienna from a stroke at the age of 22. Doubts about the Providence that could allow such an irrational tragedy were linked in the poem to wider uncertainty. Science seemed to show that nature was not benevolent, but 'red in tooth and claw'; evolution cried, 'A thousand types are gone: I care for nothing, all shall go.'[41] Nature is independent of the observer: it continues regardless of Hallam's death.

> Unwatched, the garden bough shall sway,
> The tender blossom flutter down,
> Unloved, that beech will gather brown,
> This maple burn itself away.[42]

At the end of the poem, the poet is saved from despair by a religious intimation of the presence of his friend, but the resolution is a precarious one. In his last major work, *Idylls of the King* (1859–74), Tennyson turned to the mythical past, using the break-up of Arthur's Round Table as an allegory for the Victorian loss of moral values. The cycle culminates in a tournament where the court's degeneracy is associated with mist, rain, and the dissolution of reality itself.

Towards the end of the century, one main trend of poetry was moving away from objective reality altogether into the man-made aestheticism of art for art's sake. On the other hand George Meredith, notably in *The Woods of Westermaine* (1883), evoked a nature that was hostile to man unless he placed himself in harmony with the created world. For Gerard Manley Hopkins, writing *The Wreck of the Deutschland* (1876), this harmony came through religious faith: to the five shipwrecked nuns drowning off Bremen, their agony was part of the stress that runs through all creation and, accepted, reveals the nature of God. In the sight of the watching Christ, 'Storm flakes were scroll-leaved flowers, lily showers – sweet heaven was astrew in them'.[43] In his sonnet to a falcon, 'The Windhover' (1877), he sees the battle against the wind revealing its inner beauty and being. 'The world is charged with the grandeur of God', he wrote. 'It will flame out, like shining from shook foil.'[44]

But Hopkins was unpublished until 1918, and unknown to the Victorian reading public. Nineteenth-century rural literature reaches a natural culmination and transition in Hardy. Hardy's childhood in and around Bockhampton laid the foundation of a sense of natural beauty and the seasons which may be compared, in its depth, with that of Wordsworth. Hardy's Dorset was largely untouched by modern developments, and even the town of Dorchester which, when he travelled there as an architect's pupil, boasted railways, telegraphs, and daily London newspapers only accentuated the isolation of the villages but a few miles away, where the new 'improvements' still appeared as strange and wonderful.[45] Yet, unlike the lonely hills of the Lake District, Dorset was well populated, and its landscape was a working one, shaped by centuries of agriculture, inhabited by communities living by ancient traditions. It was a palimpsest of history, shaped by generations of farmers going back to the Romans and beyond. In one world Hardy could include kinds of landscape differentiated both by appearance and by their precise impact on those who made a living from them – the rich orchard country of *Under the Greenwood Tree* (1872) and *The Woodlanders* (1887); the wild heath in *The Return of the Native* (1878); the rich pastures of the Vale of Dairies and the bleak, flinty turnip fields of Flintcomb Ash in *Tess of the d'Urbervilles* (1891).

Hardy therefore could bring together a deep poetic sense of nature with an immediate understanding of the issues of evolution and history that so disturbed Tennyson. The juxtaposition between an individual's aspirations and the impersonality of the natural processes that appear indifferent to man was not a philosophical question, but immediate experience. As Raymond Williams has written, 'Hardy thus achieves a fullness which is quite new, at this depth, in all country writing, the love and the work, the aches of labour and of choice, are in a single dimension.[46] Hardy's fiction and poetry contain many deliberately composed landscapes; yet, because they are the setting for the lives of country people, their beauty or oppressiveness comes from their working significance. The inhospitable heath of *Return of the Native* dwarfs and frustrates the romantic aspirations of Eustacia Vye; the flat cornfields stretching around Casterbridge, with its straight Roman roads, is the integral setting for Henchard's uncompromising tragedy which brings together his failures in both personal life and in corn trading.

In this context the 'picturesque' view of the countryside is questioned, not because it is outdated, but because it offers unjustified expectations. 'Men have oftener suffered from the mockery of a place too smiling than from the oppression of surroundings oversadly tinged.'[47] As Hardy's successive works deepened in their pessimism, the sense of man's inevitable tragedy existed alongside a sense of an objective reality of nature from which man, by education, self-consciousness, and changes in agriculture and rural society, was alienated. Hardy is thus profoundly a transitional figure. His power comes from the tension within his writing between early nineteenth-century romantic and modernist concerns.[48] His poem, 'The Darkling Thrust', written in 1900, deliberately invites comparisons with Keats's 'Ode to a Nightingale'. He cannot accept Keats's assumption of eternal natural beauty. Yet he is moved by the 'happy good-night air' to think that in nature there was

> Some blessed Hope, whereof he knew
> And I was unaware.

Notes

1 Emerson, 1887, 13.
2 Gilpin, 1798, 328; Gilpin, 1786, xix.
3 *Northanger Abbey*, ch. 14.
4 *Pride and Prejudice*, ch. 18.
5 *Tom Jones*, ch. 3.
6 ibid., ch. 4.
7 Duckworth, 1971, 38–54, conveniently brings together the themes of 'estate improvement' in the novel.
8 *Mansfield Park*, ch. 6.
9 ibid., ch. 20.
10 Gilpin, 1782; see also Bloomfield, 1803.
11 Wordsworth preface to *Lyrical Ballads*, 2nd edn, 1800.
12 ibid.
13 Mill, 1873, ch. 5.
14 'Mark Rutherford', *Autobiography*, 2nd edn, 1888, 18–19.
15 ibid., 1888, ch. 1.
16 Arnold, 1879, 293–4 (Everyman edn, 1964).
17 Bloomfield, 1803, xxxvi–vii.
18 Clare, 1827, 'January'.
19 ibid., 'March'.
20 Tibble, 1935, II, 447–8.
21 Jones, 1962, 736–7 (W. Barnes, 'Come and Meet Me').
22 Tibble, 1935, II, 559–67.
23 Ricks, 1969, 1123, 1189–91 (Tennyson, 'Northern Farmer, Old Style' and 'Northern Farmer, New Style').

24 Jones, 1962, I (2), 532.
25 Tibble, 1935, I, 36.
26 Elliott, 1829, I, stanza 12.
27 ibid., X, stanza 9.
28 Andrews, 1888–9.
29 Brightfield, 1968, I, 550–1.
30 See, for example, Thomas, 1978, ch. 6.
31 Gaskell, 1857.
32 Knoepflmacher and Tennyson, 1977, 391–425, gives a convenient summary of the issues.
33 Cook and Wedderburn, 1903, III, 623–4.
34 Williams, 1973, especially chs 16–18.
35 G. Levine in Knoepflmacher and Tennyson, 1977, 137–52.
36 *Adam Bede* (1859), *Silas Marner* (1861), and *Felix Holt* (1866) are Eliot's novels which most centrally use the possibilities of a historically distanced landscape, although she sets other of her fiction in the past.
37 Arnold, *The Scholar Gipsy*, stanza xxi.
38 John Stephens (Frederick George Stephens), 'The Purpose and Tendency of Early Italian Art', *Germ*, no. 2, 58–64.
39 For example, Hunt, 1886, 740.
40 For a discussion of the impact of pre-Darwinian evolutionary theory on English social life see Gillispie, 1951; Henkin, 1963; Knoepflmacher and Tennyson, 1977, 216–30.
41 *In Memoriam*, stanza 56.
42 ibid., stanza 101.
43 G. M. Hopkins, *The Wreck of the Deutschland*, stanza 21.
44 Hopkins, 'God's Grandeur'.
45 Williams, 1973, ch. 18; Williams, 1972, pt II.
46 Williams, 1972, 212.
47 Hardy, *Return of the Native* (1878), book I, ch. 1.
48 For Hardy's concern with the issues raised by evolution see, for example, Knoepflmacher and Tennyson, 1977, 259–77.

6

The land in Victorian literature

W. J. Keith

A country's literature does not necessarily reflect the historical actualities of the time in which it is written, since writers are influenced by conventions and the traditional practices and expectations of their art as well as by what they see around them. Such conventional forms as pastoral and Gothic romance, for example, may well coexist with realistic presentation and so distort the historical record. Thus readers of Matthew Arnold's 'Thyrsis' or Emily Brontë's *Wuthering Heights* would be unwise to assume that scholar gypsies might be seen on the Cumnor Hills in the nineteenth century or that Heathcliffs habitually roamed the Yorkshire moors. None the less, the Victorian age belongs to what Northrop Frye has called the 'low mimetic' period of literary history, dominated by middle-class values that favoured a realistic art.[1] Consequently, so long as we proceed with caution, Victorian literature can foster and augment our understanding of nineteenth-century attitudes towards the countryside.

Descriptions and evocations of the land abound in the literature of this period, and this profusion of reference dramatically underlines the fact that 'land' is a word embracing numerous shades of meaning. For many Victorians it was automatically associated with concepts of possession and, by extension, of power. A great estate presupposed a great man who owned it. Perhaps because, after the first Reform Act (1832), the landed rural gentry was losing its political dominance over the country as a whole, the continued influence of local families on rural parishes became a favourite subject in fiction, where they could provoke a wide range of responses extending from nostalgic sympathy through ironic amusement to indignant satire. But despite what we can now recognize as the trend of the times, land was generally associated with a sense of permanence and security. Trollope's Barchester series achieved (and has maintained) its popularity not only because of his wittily human presentation of church politics but because of his congenial portrayal of a society which, although threatened by various forces from without, retained an inner strength and basic stability. 'The greatness of Barchester', Trollope writes in the first chapter of *Doctor Thorne*, 'depends wholly on the landed powers', and this is one of many Victorian novels (George Eliot's *Felix Holt* is another) in which the plot turns upon the inheritance of a large estate. The power of land can be used for good or evil, its possessors may prove heroes or villains, but its importance (in the abstract) remains paramount.

This attitude to land favours a panoramic view of rural life, the Victorian equivalent of the eighteenth-century 'prospect' from the high ground in a gentleman's park. Again, the opening paragraphs of *Doctor Thorne* provide a convenient example. Barsetshire is described as

> a county in the west of England not so full of life, indeed, nor so widely spoken of as some of its manufacturing leviathan brethren in the north, but which is, nevertheless, very dear to those who know it well. Its green pastures, its waving wheat, its deep and shady and – let us add – dirty lanes, its paths and stiles, its tawny-coloured, well-built rural churches, its avenues of beeches, and frequent Tudor mansions, its constant county hunt, its social graces, and the general air of clanship which pervades it, has made it to its own inhabitants a favoured land of Goshen. It is purely agricultural; agricultural in its produce, agricultural in its poor, and agricultural in its pleasures.[2]

One wonders, however, whether the working farmers and labourers of Barsetshire would have seen the country in quite this way. For them 'land' and 'earth' become virtually synonymous. The dirt in the lanes, that Trollope mentions self-consciously and with seeming reluctance, becomes central: it is the soil upon which their livelihood depends. In a well-known passage from *Tess of the d'Urbervilles*, Thomas Hardy presents the land from a very different perspective:

> The swede-field in which [Tess] and her companion were set hacking was a stretch of a hundred odd acres, in one patch, on the highest ground of the farm, rising above stony lanchets or lynchets. . . . The upper half of each turnip had been eaten off by the live-stock, and it was the business of the two women to grub up the lower or earthy half of the root with a hooked fork called a hacker, that it might be eaten also. Every leaf of the vegetable having already been consumed, the whole field was in colour a desolate drab; it was a complexion without features, as if a face, from chin to brow, should be only an expanse of skin. The sky wore, in another colour, the same likeness; a white vacuity of countenance with the lineaments gone. So these two upper and nether visages confronted each other all day long, the white face looking down on the brown face, and the brown face looking up at the white face, without anything standing between them but the two girls crawling over the surface of the former like flies.[3]

The face of the countryside, then, alters with the perspective from which it is viewed. The land can be a thing of beauty, but also a hard taskmaster. Richard Jefferies, describing a harvest scene in his essay 'One of the New Voters' (*The Open Air*), catches the range of possible response in a single sentence: 'The wheat is beautiful, but human life is labour.'[4]

Trollope's claim that Barsetshire was '*to its own inhabitants* a favoured land of Goshen' is difficult to accept; but most of Trollope's readers, and most readers of other rural literature, were outsiders with no immediate experience of agriculture, and for them the vision of an idyllic countryside proved attractive. It is impossible to over-emphasize the fact that, by half way through Victoria's reign, the majority of the population lived and worked in towns. Understandably, most urban Victorian readers turned to rural literature for the same reasons that they sought the countryside itself – for refreshment and renewal, as a haven from the wearying pace of city life. The usual adjective for such motives, 'escapist', carries negative connotations, but the practice is not (or, rather, need not be) ignoble. A distinction needs to be made between two very different kinds of escape usefully indicated by two of Hardy's novel titles: escape to (*Under the Greenwood Tree*) and escape from (*Far from the Madding Crowd*). The former almost invariably overlaps with pastoral, the positing of a 'golden world' or never-never land remote from what Arnold called, in 'The Scholar Gipsy',

> this strange disease of modern life,
> With its sick hurry, its divided aims,
> Its heads o'ertaxed, its palsied hearts (ll. 203–5)

'Escape from' does not imply inferior art, but the value of that art as historical evidence is negligible. This kind of escape is prominent in the novels of Dickens: Dingley Dell in *The Pickwick Papers* provides the most obvious example, its very name suggesting a sheltered warmth and simplicity, but many others could be cited, including the cottage to which Nell and her grandfather come near the close of *The Old Curiosity Shop*, and Betsy Trotwood's home by 'the sacred piece of green' and Peggotty's quaint boat on the beach in *David Copperfield*. Such localities are less important for their own sakes than for their functions as opposite poles to an urban threat typified by Blake's 'dark Satanic Mills' or, more substantially, by William Cobbett's 'great Wen'.

'Escape to' is more positive. The urban readerof George Eliot's *Adam Bede* may first approach the village of Hayslope as if it were a pastoral retreat (once again the name is comfortably lulling), but he quickly discovers that he is confronted here with a community presented in breadth and depth, an alternative way of life which is of interest in its own right. He is introduced not to a world of pastoral ease but to an active society engaged in rural labour. George Eliot offers a remarkably comprehensive view of village life from Squire Donnithorne through the farming Poysers to the artisans like Adam Bede himself. The novel examines the cohesiveness of a rural community, the responsibility of each member to the complete human unit. In writing the book, George Eliot saw herself as a pioneer, presenting realistic truth where her predecessors had offered selective glimpses which led to falsehood. 'I find a source of delicious sympathy', she confides, 'in these faithful pictures of a monotonous homely existence.'[5] Twentieth-century readers, however, are likely to consider the idyllic aspects of Hayslope overstressed. Accustomed to Hardy's Wessex and the dark vision so congenial to the modern mind, we tend to find the landscapes of 'Loamshire' too idealized and simplistic; where, we feel obliged to ask, is the grinding poverty which social historians assure us was widespread? But George Eliot, whatever her omissions, was feeling towards that sense of regional consciousness which is so important and neglected a development in the Victorian period. Advances in communications, the improvement of roads, and the establishment of the railway system, had 'opened up' the countryside for exploration and comparison. The Victorians, we might say, learned to recognize not a generalized countryside but a series of different countrysides with their own physical features, history, customs, dialects, and ways of living. The Victorian writers, whether of poetry, fiction, or discursive prose, had an important role to play in this awakening.

Fifteen years before Victoria ascended the throne, William Cobbett initiated his *Rural Rides* (published as a book in 1830) as follows: 'My object was, not to see inns and turnpike-roads, but to see the *country*; to see the farmers at *home*, and to see the labourers in the fields.'[6] He confined his attention, for the most part, to southern England, and so missed the opportunity of observing and commenting on the more dramatic scenic differences in countrysides. Moreover, his socio-political concerns – a major part of his interest – were always in the forefront. None the less, he provides an invaluable record of differences between county and county, differences determined ultimately by the nature of the soil, which in turn affected the kind of agriculture possible in the area, which in its turn influenced the material condition of the inhabitants. Cobbett's viewpoint was essentially that of the practical countryman; he judged the land according to what it produced or could produce, and had little patience with those who looked at the countryside aesthetically or regarded it as a place for relaxation. Such, however, fostered by the 'romantic' taste for wild nature, was a trend of the times, and later writers were to describe, assess, and interpret the countryside for the prospering urbanized middle class (or, in Cobbett's contemptuous terminology, 'the tax-eaters').

A far less important but doubtless more representative writer, William

Howitt, produced his panoramic survey, *The Rural Life of England*, in 1838. He explains his intentions in the preface:

> My object in this volume has been to present to the reader a view of the Rural Life of England at the present period, as seen in all classes and in all parts of the country. For this purpose I have not merely depended upon my acquaintance with rural life, which has been that of a great portion of my own life from boyhood, but I have literally travelled, and a great deal of it on foot, from the Land's End to the Tweed, penetrating into the retirements, and witnessing the domestic life of the country in primitive seclusions and under rustic roofs.[7]

Howitt writes in full awareness of the new audience for his work. He notes that 'one of the singular features of English life at the present moment is the swarming of summer tourists in all interesting quarters',[8] and later exclaims:

> And what an immensity of new regions will the railroads that are now beginning to stretch their lines from the metropolis in different directions, lay open – *terraei incognitae*, as it were, to the millions that in the dense and ever-growing mass of monstrous London pant after an outburst into the country.[9]

Howitt was both an enthusiast and a sentimentalist: 'The wealth and refinement at which this country has arrived, have thrown round English rural life every possible charm.'[10] Although evidence of poverty and degradation among the poor are to be found in his book, these are for the most part offset by complacent generalities about improvement. His middle-class presuppositions are obvious: 'When we go into the cottage of the working man, how forcibly are we struck with the difference between his mode of life and our own,'[11] and his rather desperate attempts to equate the evidence of his senses with the 'pastoral' poetic tradition prove revealing: 'In many of the southern counties, but I think nowhere more than in Hampshire, do the cottages realize, in my view, every conception that our poets have given us of them.'[12] Howitt writes about everything he encounters, including country sports, scientific farming, farm servants, gypsies, cottage life, and education in rural areas. Although his observations are limited by his naïvety, they remain useful in providing a comprehensive and perhaps typically Victorian view of the English countryside.

Howitt's treatment of rural sports reminds us that for many Victorians the countryside was a place not for rest and idle relaxation but for strenuous activity, especially in the forms of hunting and shooting. While many rural commentators indulged in nostalgia for a supposedly simpler past, others looked back to a past that was tougher and more virile. For George Borrow the gypsies, prizefighters, horse traders, tinkers, jockeys, and roadgirls about whom he wrote represented a sturdy, 'free' England that was fast being superseded by a Victorianism of effeminate pseudo-gentility. In *The Romany Rye*, a sequel to his better-known *Lavengro*, he speaks of 'the wholesome smell of the stable with which many of these pages are redolent'.[13] We have become so accustomed to the stereotype of a Victorian England dominated by Mrs Grundy and the dictates of respectability that we can easily overlook the more vigorous and less inhibited worlds to which numerous youthful Victorians were able (at least temporarily) to 'escape'.

Nowhere is this aspect of the Victorian period better evoked than in the words of R. S. Surtees. The emphasis here is not merely on ''untin', to employ the idiom of his great creation John Jorrocks, the cockney master of foxhounds, but on the vital but rather seedy world of horse traders, stable boys, and all the sporting observers and hangers on. Jorrocks himself, though it sounds pompous to say so, takes on the status of a symbol. As London tea merchant he represents that urban enthusiasm for rural pursuits about which Howitt wrote, but he is also a new social phenomenon: the self-made cockney who can infiltrate a sport hitherto dominated by the rural squirearchy. Surtees's ambivalent response to his creation is also significant; he laughs at Jorrocks's ignorance and vulgarity, and makes him a figure of fun whenever he can (in *Handley Cross* Jorrocks falls into 'the dirtiest heap of composition for turnips I ever smelt in my life'),[14] but at the same time Surtees used him to show up the snobbery and conceit of more typical huntsmen and to express some of his own cherished convictions. Surtees was himself a rural landowner, but there is a bluff heartiness and honesty in Jorrocks that he finds endearing. Moreover, although there are few pages of formal description in his books, we gain from them a unique view of the country as seen on horseback from the covert-side, and, particularly, the winter landscape of the foxhunting season rather than the summer of tourists and holiday-makers.

Surtees's best-known works (*Handley Cross, Mr Sponge's Sporting Tour, Mr Facey Romford's Hounds*) are officially categorized as novels. But the temporal and causal development central to the art of fiction is not present, and they are continually breaking up into sketches and character vignettes. His contemporary readers were interested not so much in his art as in his subject-matter, not so much in plot progression as in individual scenes and human types. This is a characteristic of rural literature partly explicable in terms of the country writer's dislike of falsification and his commitment to a representative truth. The distinction between fiction and non-ficion is less pronounced here; Surtees's non-fictional *Analysis of the Hunting Field*, with its series of chapters devoted to 'The Master', 'The Huntsman', 'The Whipper-In', 'The Earth-Stopper', and so on, bears a closer resemblance to his novels than we might at first expect. The modern reader can find, in novel and essay alike, authentic presentations of rural scenes and rural people.

Richard Jefferies, our best literary guide to gamekeeping, poaching, and shooting, discovered his appropriate art form in the rural essay at the same time as he found his true subject matter. After numerous and generally dismal attempts at novel writing, he published *The Gamekeeper at Home* in 1878, the first of a series of country books in which information about rural things is tactfully interspersed with vivid evocation of the ways of country life. The average urban sportsman who could devote no more than a week or so to his recreation found in Jefferies's work what he most needed: articles on choosing a gun, accounts of pheasant rearing, information about natural history, portraits of typical countrymen and a general accumulation of advice about rural things as well as personal accounts of his own experiences in the field which many a frustrated urbanite must have read with a combination of enjoyment and envy. Moreover, the numerous books that flowed from his pen in the decade before his untimely death in 1887 – books with such attractive titles as *Wild Life in a Southern County, The Amateur Poacher, The Life of the Fields, The Open Air* – offered the essence of the countryside in book form, works to be cherished and re-read when urban duties prevented the reader's presence in the countryside about which Jefferies wrote. But his most ambitious work of this kind is *Hodge and His Masters*, a commentary on the agricultural state of the country at a time when the 'high farming' of mid-century was giving place to grim years of agricultural depression. Jefferies made his point by means of a series of minutely observed character sketches of farmers, labourers, and countrymen. In no other rural work, perhaps, is the human vitality of the Victorian countryside more thoroughly and cogently presented.

'The beauty of English woodland and country lies in its detail', Jefferies wrote in 'An English Deer-Park' (*Field and Hedgerow*). Certainly, his own success at evoking the spirit of a countryside (as distinct from merely amassing facts) stems from his capacity to select and arrange significant details with all the skill of an impressionist painter. A single extract, from *Round About a Great Estate*, must suffice to illustrate his gift for transcending description and communicating what it feels like to move within a specific countryside (in this case, north Wiltshire):

> Upon reaching the foot of the Downs, Cicely left the highway and entered a narrow lane without hedges, but worn low between banks of chalk or white rubble. The track was cut up with ruts so deep that the bed of the pony-trap seemed almost to touch the ground. As we went rather slowly along this awkward place we could see the wild thyme growing on the bank at the side. Presently we got on the slope of the hill, and at the summit passed the entrenchment. . . . Thence our track

> ran along the ridge, on the short sweet turf, where there were few or no ruts, and these easily avoided on that broad open ground. The quick pony now put on his speed, and we raced along as smoothly as if the wheels were running on a carpet. Far below, to the right, stretched wheatfield after wheatfield in a plain between two ridges of hills. On the opposite slope, a mile away, came the shadows of the clouds – then down along the corn towards us. Stonechats started from the flints and low bushes as we went by; an old crow – it is always an old crow – rose hastily from behind a fence of withered thorn, and a magpie fluttered down the hill to the fields beneath, where was a flock of sheep. The breeze at this height made the sunshine pleasant.[15]

In Jefferies, informed countryman and creative artist merge. The authoritative references, the range of sense-impressions, the wealth of rural knowledge upon which such a passage depends, are easy to recognize; more difficult to appreciate is the subtle modulation of sounds and rhythms that give the paragraph its grace and eloquence without disturbing the conversational intimacy of the tone. Here the land is recreated by the art that conceals art.

Descriptive accounts of rural England in the nineteenth century run the gamut from formal statistical surveys to artistic evocations of rural scenes in the manner of Jefferies. They include works that emphasize, for example, natural history, country crafts, the social conditions of the labourer, and the pastimes of the ruling class. These are too numerous to consider here, but mention needs to be made of H. Rider Haggard's *Rural England*. Haggard was an enthusiastic and conscientious gentleman-farmer who used his profits from such exotic fiction as *King Solomon's Mines* and *She* to farm his Norfolk estate. He saw Arthur Young, the late eighteenth-century advocate of land improvement, as his 'great predecessor',[16] but for our purposes his book performs a similar function at the time of Queen Victoria's death to that of Cobbett's *Rural Rides* a few years before she ascended the throne.

Like Cobbett, Haggard is conducting an inquiry into the state of agricultural England. He is concerned to examine the dramatic changes that had recently taken place in farming methods, to assess the consequences of the agricultural depression over the previous twenty years, and to gauge the prospects for the immediate future. He favours the method of the interview, which preserves 'an actual record of what a certain number of people intimately connected with English land and agriculture, thought and said on the matter in the years 1901 and 1902'.[17] Conscious of the extreme variation of conditions from region to region, he organizes his material by counties, and makes a systematic attempt to compare and contrast the state of one area with that of others. Haggard's position as landowner naturally results in a viewpoint very different from Cobbett's, and his clear but unimaginative prose contrasts with the earlier writer's pugnaciously forceful style. Fact and interpretation can be disentangled more readily in *Rural England*, but we do not receive that acutely vivid sense of an observed countryside that is so palpable an effect in *Rural Rides*. None the less, Haggard makes an honest attempt to present divergent opinions. He was assisted in his chapter on Dorset by Thomas Hardy, and his book has a special interest in offering a contemporary non-fiction equivalent to the fictional re-creation of a Victorian countryside in Hardy's Wessex novels.

Hardy's writings (the poems and non-fiction prose as well as the novels and short stories) clearly constitute the most important comprehensive presentation in literature of the nineteenth-century countryside. Its local concentration on an area of south-west England (the artistic culmination of the development of regional consciousness discussed earlier) is less limiting than one might expect. Wessex extends over the boundaries of nine modern counties and embraces a rich variety of kinds of countryside from coastal areas to bare upland to sheltered and fertile vales. Human habitations range from the county town of Casterbridge/Dorchester through seaside resorts and several cathedral cities to widely divergent villages, hamlets, isolated farms, and cottages. Wessex is, in fact, a rural microcosm, and as novelistic chronicler Hardy covers the broad time-span of the whole nineteenth century from the Napoleonic invasion scare of 1804 in *The Trumpet-Major* to the bleakly contemporary world of *Jude the Obscure*.

Hardy was in a unique position to represent this countryside in all its detail and complexity. The successful man of letters who wrote his later novels at Max Gate, the solid, gauntly contoured Victorian house he built for himself just outside Dorchester in the 1880s, had been born in 1840 in a small, 'picturesque' but decidely cramped cottage a few miles away at Bockhampton on the outskirts of 'Egdon Heath'. Though his father was a mason and contractor, many of his local relatives, as Robert Gittings has recently demonstrated in *Young Thomas Hardy*,[18] belonged to the labouring class – a fact that Hardy himself, sharing the social sensitivity of so many Victorians, took considerable pains to conceal. Fortunate in his own education, he moved from Bockhampton to Dorchester, and later to London, broadening his social and intellectual horizons as he went. When he became known as a novelist, he moved (rather awkwardly) in high social circles, and his autobiographical notes are strewn with references to society dinners and titled acquaintances. Though he was never altogether at ease in portraying the upper classes, his experience enabled him to draw upon a broad social range of rural figures from Mrs Charmond, the lady of the manor in *The Woodlanders*, and the parvenu Stoke-d'Urbervilles in *Tess*, to characters like Jude Fawley and Tess herself.

Hardy *knew* the countryside about which he wrote from all the viewpoints that I have outlined. And he was acutely conscious of the increasing split between rural and urban in his own age. He could see Wessex through the eyes of the humbly born and intellectually ambitious Jude, eager to escape from the constrictions of his environment; but he could also see it, as a native who had himself returned, through the eyes of Clym Yeobright. He shared the inner knowledge of the realities of rural living that makes his presentations of the poorer countrymen so convincing, but he could also understand the responses of outsiders who came to Wessex and found difficulty in adjusting to local ways. He realized that he lived in two time-schemes; as he wrote in *Far from the Madding Crowd*: 'The citizen's *Then* is the rustic's *Now*. . . . In these Wessex nooks the busy outsider's ancient times are only old; his old times are still new; his present is futurity'.[19] He inherited many of the traditional attitudes of the rural population, yet learnt to come to terms with the up-to-date intellectual controversies of the metropolis. He understood, too, that his readers were, for the most part, these same citizens and busy outsiders eager to explore his countryside as tourists: hence the topographical emphasis of the prefaces and introductions that he later wrote for his novels.

All this biographical and social background is necessary, I believe, for an adequate appreciation of the subtleties of Hardy's presentation of 'land'. His landscapes vary dramatically, but in nearly all of them we encounter a distinct sense of unease. This is particularly evident, of course, in Hardy's best-known word-portrait of a tract of country, the description of Egdon Heath in the opening chapter of *The Return of the Native*. We are told that 'civilization was its enemy' but also that it was 'a spot which returned upon the memory of those who loved it with an aspect of peculiar and kindly congruity'. It is 'haggard Egdon', 'a near relation of night', 'the hitherto unrecognized original of those wild regions of obscurity which are vaguely felt to be compassing us about in midnight dreams of flight and disaster'. Yet it is also offered as 'a place perfectly accordant with man's nature – neither ghastly, hateful, nor ugly; neither commonplace, unmeaning, nor tame; but, like man, slighted and enduring'.[20] These are not contradictions; they represent Hardy's most deliberate statement concerning the relation between man and his landscape – or, in more specific terms, between Victorian man and the Victorian landscape.

This same sense of awkwardness and unease recurs, less directly but no less significantly, in other novels. In *The Mayor of Casterbridge*, for example, 'the Ring', a Roman amphitheatre where natural features have been adapted by man to provide a background for human violence through the ages, becomes a suitable meeting-place for Michael Henchard and the wife that he has wronged;[21] the historical associations of the locality are invoked to colour the nineteenth-century human story being played out against it. Frequently, landscape descriptions clash dramatically within a single novel. In *Far from the Madding Crowd* idyllic presentations of sheep-dipping and sheep-shearing stand in contrast to the memorable scene of violent thunderstorm in which Gabriel and Bathsheba fight to save the wheat ricks from the destructive force of the elements. And in *Tess* the quiet lush beauty of the dairy country at Talbothays is deliberately set against the harsh barrenness of Flintcomb Ash.

Hardy's Wessex is a region undergoing radical and painful change. This can often be seen within the landscape itself (Farfrae's mechanical seed drill in *The Mayor of Casterbridge*, which will 'revolutionize sowing heer-about',[22] the Stoke-d-Urbervilles' newly constructed 'country-house built for enjoyment pure and simple, with not an acre of troublesome land attached to it' and the 'red tyrant' of the threshing machine in *Tess*),[23] and it is paralleled in the uncomfortable and uncertain lives of Hardy's characters. Hardy has often been criticized in the past for his unskilful juxtapositions of documentary reporting and artificial melodrama; but we are coming to realize more and more that the awkward shifts of tone within the novels both reflect and reproduce the jagged patterns of modern experience. In the preface to *Far from the Madding Crowd* Hardy insisted that he was presenting 'a Wessex population living under Queen Victoria; – a modern Wessex of railways, the penny-post, mowing and reaping machines, union workhouses, lucifer matches, labourers who could read and write, and National school children'.[24] Once again the incongruous juxtapositions are noticeable. All in all, Hardy's Wessex novels, read as a series and backed up by his other writings in prose and verse, constitute a profound analysis as well as an unrivalled representation of nineteenth-century rural life and landscape.

Commentators who have grown impatient with the rural positives frequently talk of an idealizing rural 'myth' which distorts and falsifies the darker rural 'reality'. To what extent can such a response be justified? There is, of course, no simple answer to this question. In any age the temptation to idealize is strong, and the Victorian period was no exception. As Bulwer Lytton remarked, 'we can have our real life, in all its harsh outlines, whenever we please; we do not want to see that real life, but its ideal image, in the fable land of art'.[25] It is only too easy, moreover, to fall back upon literary stereotypes. Mrs Gaskell neatly illustrates this in *North and South* when Margaret Hale, discussing a village in which she used to live, says, 'I am trying to describe Helstone as it really is', but goes on to remark that it is 'like a village in a poem – in one of Tennyson's poems'.[26]

On the other hand, the argument that Victorian literature as a whole offers an excessively rosy picture of contemporary rural life can only be maintained by a selection of evidence as distorting as the supposed idealizing myth itself. Indeed, the presentation of a countryside 'as it really is' is a major preoccupation of nineteenth-century rural writing, and although some of the attempts may have been no more successful than that of Mrs Gaskell's heroine, many are harsh indeed. This is especially true, of course, of the social novels of the period that deal with specifically rural themes. Here, for example, is a passage from Disraeli's *Sybil*:

> The situation of the rural town of Marney was one of the most delightful easily to be imagined. In a spreading dale contiguous to the margin of a clear and lively stream, surrounded by meadows and gardens, and backed by lofty hills, undulating and richly wooded, the traveller on the opposite heights of the dale would often stop to admire the merry prospect that recalled to him the traditonal epithet of his country.
>
> Beautiful illusion! For behind that laughing landscape, penury and disease fed upon the vitals of a miserable population.[27]

Similarly, when Lancelot Smith in Charles Kingsley's *Yeast* maintains that 'wherever one goes one sees commodious new cottages springing up', the radical gamekeeper Tregarva replies:

> 'Wherever you go, sir, but what of wherever you don't go? Along the roadsides and round the gentlemen's parks, where the cottages are in sight, it's all very smart; but just go into the outlying hamlets – a whited sepulchre, sir, is many a great estate.'[28]

Tennyson, stressing behaviour rather than material conditions, expressed comparable sentiments through the speaker of *Maud*:

> Below me, there, is the village, and looks how quiet and small!
> And yet bubbles o'er like the city, with gossip, scandal and spite.
> (ll. 108–9)

Perhaps because the temptation to idealize is so strong and the accusation of it so easy, writers are particularly sensitive on this issue. At any rate, disclaimers are frequent. Even Hardy, for instance, in his 'General Preface to the Novels and Poems' written for the Wessex edition of 1912, felt the need to insist: 'At the dates represented in the various narrations things were like that in Wessex.'

Myths regularly provoke counter-myths. The pastoral tradition, in substituting Arcadia or Eden for the realities of country life, is not likely to pass unchallenged for long, but the concentration upon squalor and misery need be no more accurate than an emphasis on charm and ease. By the same token, Wordsworth's 'natural comfort'[29] is qualified but not cancelled by Tennyson's 'Nature red in tooth and claw'.[30] The evidence of literature will admittedly include extremes but it will also offer balance. Once again, Hardy's Tess, ambiguously called 'a pure woman' in the subtitle, provides the complexity of truth. The Tess whom we know and respect by the end of the novel is neither the embodiment of rustic innocence imagined by

Angel Clare before their marriage nor the type of guilty impostor that he projects upon her after she has told him her story. If we read *Tess of the d'Urbervilles* symbolically (which is, of course, only a partial interpretation of the novel's total effect), we can see Tess, torn between the frigidly angelic Clare and the callously satanic d'Urberville, as representative of the middle state of ordinary human nature. And, as we have seen, the landscape in which she moves, the extremes of Talbothays and Flintcomb Ash, reflects this human duality.

The variety possible within literature mirrors the variety within nature and the multiplicity of attitudes, in the Victorian period or any other, towards the land. Examples may be found in the most unexpected places. One would not normally think of invoking Oscar Wilde as a commentator on the Victorian countryside, but in his love for turning hallowed ideas and commonplaces upside down he should not be ignored. In *The Importance of Being Earnest*, he makes Lady Bracknell observe, while interviewing a suitor for her daughter's hand, 'A girl with a simple, unspoiled nature, like Gwendolyn, can hardly be expected to reside in the country.'[31] The humour lies in the reversal of customary assumptions, but it still makes its point (Wilde may even have had the current controversy over Hardy's Tess in mind). And paradoxically this master of paradoxes provides an excellent digest of the changes in historical and social attitudes to 'land' in the late nineteenth century. What at first appears a succession of witty epigrams comes to be recognized as significant insight into contemporary trends. It is therefore appropriate to leave the last word with Lady Bracknell:

> What between the duties expected of one during one's lifetime, and the duties extracted from one after one's death, land has ceased to be either a profit or a pleasure. It gives one position, and prevents one from keeping it up. That's all that can be said about land.[32]

Notes

1 Frye, 1957.
2 Trollope [1858], 1957.
3 Hardy [1891], 1974, ch. 43.
4 Jefferies [1885], 1948.
5 Eliot [1859], 1951, ch. 17.
6 Cobbett [1830], 1967.
7 Howitt [1838], 1844, viii.
8 ibid., 37.
9 ibid., 556–7.
10 ibid., 11.
11 ibid., 404.
12 ibid., 411.
13 Borrow [1857], 1907, ch. 25.
14 Surtees [1843], 1926, ch. 10.

15 Jefferies [1880], 1948, ch. 10.
16 Haggard, 1902, I, vii.
17 ibid., I, xi.
18 Gittings, 1975.
19 Hardy [1874], 1974, ch. 22.
20 Hardy [1878], 1974, ch. 1.
21 Hardy [1886], 1974, ch. 11.
22 ibid., ch. 24.
23 Hardy [1891], 1974, chs 5 and 47.
24 Hardy [1874], 1974.
25 Quoted in Stang, 1959, 155.
26 Gaskell [1855], 1925, ch. 1.
27 Disraeli [1845], 1954, bk II, ch. 3.
28 Kingsley [1850], 1881, ch. 13.
29 See *The Excursion*, I, 602, in *Poetical Works of Wordsworth*, 1960.
30 *In Memoriam*, LVI, 15, in Ricks, 1972.
31 Wilde [1895], 1961, Act I.
32 ibid.

7

A planned countryside

Alan Rogers

The English countryside has changed very substantially both in form and function since the beginning of this century. Despite the commonly-held view that the countryside is unchanging, it is arguable that it has seen at least as much physical and social change as have the urban areas since 1900. This chapter reviews the extent and nature of that change from the viewpoint of the use of land, while the following one considers the changes which have occurred to the population of the rural areas.

Two major interrelated themes can be seen to stand out in overviewing changes in the land use structure of the countryside since the turn of the century. The first has been the concern to conserve the countryside as the arena for activities which are supposedly natural rather than constructed, and which often involve 'traditional' land uses such as agriculture and forestry. The demands to conserve the rural areas and to limit countryside change have been every bit as strong in the twentieth century as they were in previous centuries. This clearly links with a deep-seated view of rural landscape and society which Raymond Williams noted in his classic book *The Country and the City*.[1]

A related theme must be that of state involvement and planning. The twentieth century will be recognized as the period when, albeit in different ways and with differing levels of enthusiasm, both government and governed felt strongly that the *laissez-faire* of previous times was insufficient to lead to the fulfilment of economic, social, and aesthetic objectives for the countryside.

It has been argued elsewhere[2] that there can be recognized a broad structure of three periods of radical change in twentieth-century political life as it has affected the countryside. The first, towards the end of the first decade, came from Lloyd George in the reforming Liberal administration. The second had its origins during the Second World War and was centred upon the Labour government's programme in the late 1940s. Both these periods were characterized by a concern for rural reconstruction following the ravages of economic depression and war and for planning – both in a general interventionist sense as well as, specifically, with regard to the land uses of town and country. The third period of radical change is still ongoing. It dates from the late 1970s and is associated with a Conservative administration committed to limit the influence of the state and to open up the economy to free competition. Yet the long-standing power of state involvement and planning can be seen even here. Indeed, in some senses the 'power of planning' appears even more impressive, as a supposedly anti-interventionist government is continually seen to be forced to place its reforms within a wider context of state and supra-state planning. Whether we consider the protection of the countryside (e.g. Green Belt legislation) or the reforming of agricultural policy (but within the structure of the Common Agricultural Policy), all rural policies are seen to exist within entrenched, even immovable, national and international planning structures.

Towards a planned countryside

This theme of interventionism and of state planning is, then, an important starting point in any discussion of the changing countryside in the twentieth century. The changes of land use which can be recounted have of course been consequent upon a great many factors. The growth of population, increasing affluence and wealth, the development of technology, especially transport – such factors have all played their part. But a constant component in all of this has been the hand of government seeking to plan, to influence, and to control.

This role of intervention and state planning has operated on two broad fronts. One has concerned the agricultural industry and thereby the way in which farmers use the land. The second has concerned the way in which non-agricultural land is used, whether for towns and cities, for recreation, nature conservation, or the production of minerals. At least until fairly recently, these two broad directions for planning have been kept remarkably separate. 'Town and country planners' – who grew in influence especially in the early post-war years – have been largely excluded from interfering in farming and agricultural land uses, though some have argued that land use planning powers should be extended into the farming sector.[3] They have operated mainly within urban confines, and rural matters have often been relegated to a secondary position in their professional esteem. It has been seen as a major task for these planners to protect the countryside from excessive urban incursion and thereby to leave it to its 'proper' custodians, the farmers.

Other planners have essentially been concerned with economic – rather than physical – planning. Based primarily in the Ministry of Agriculture and its extension services, they have been concerned to influence the activities of farmers so as to maintain their incomes and encourage them to produce an increasing proportion of the nation's food. The means have not been physical plans nor the requirement for a farmer to gain permission to put his land to a particular use. Rather have they been phrased in fiscal and financial terms, providing monetary incentives and subsidies to encourage production of certain foodstuffs, and thereby indirectly to influence land use.

Only in recent years can it be said that the activities of these two sets of planners have been seriously questioned to a significant extent. By the late 1970s it was increasingly realized that the encouragement of agricultural production had created an expensive and arguably too successful creature. Self-sufficiency in most temperate foodstuffs was well within sight, if not already achieved, yet the costs of financial support (not least in storing unwanted foods) had risen to astronomical heights. Moreover, farmers were increasingly being seen, not as the 'custodians' of the countryside as the wartime Scott Report had argued,[4] but as its potential destroyers, through the use of machines and chemicals leading to soil erosion, habitat destruction, the pollution of rivers and aquifers, and so on.

Town and country planners have also had their role questioned. On the one hand, some have argued that land use planning has failed in its prime objective of safeguarding agricultural land for the future.[5] More recently, however, there has grown up a view that this form of planning has actually been too restrictive and had thereby inhibited economic growth in the countryside to the detriment of the rural population and the economic revival of rural areas.

Planned support for agriculture had its origins in the 1920s and 1930s when English farming sank even lower into a depression which had begun in the 1870s.[6] The First World War had seen a brief improvement in farmers' fortunes as the country was forced to feed itself rather than depend on imports. Moreover, government promised continued financial support through the Corn Production Acts. The repeal of these in 1921 was of major long-term significance, not least in the effect which this perceived betrayal had upon the political relationship between farmers and future governments. The experiences of the 1920s and 1930s, when English farming suffered at the hands of world competition, have taken a long time to be erased. Even the partial reinstatement of support for cereal farmers in the 1932 Wheat Act did little to remove the suspicion of the farming industry towards government. In turn, it is not too much of an exaggeration to see the commitment to state support for agriculture given after the Second World War and embodied in the 1947 Agriculture Act as a determination on the part of government not to betray the wartime trust again.

The 1947 Act became the keystone to a planned agriculture, with the intention of:

> promoting and maintaining, by the provision of guaranteed markets and assured prices . . . a stable and efficient industry capable of producing such part of the nation's food and other agricultural produce as in the national interest it is desirable to produce in the United Kingdom, and of producing it at minimum prices consistent with proper remuneration and living conditions for farmers and workers in agriculture and an adequate return on capital invested in the industry.

Along with this system of 'guaranteed markets and assured prices' came a close relationship between government and the farmers in the form of regular contact with the National Farmers' Union and an annual price review. This liaison assured farmers of generally satisfactory prices and led indirectly to other advantages by way of preferential tax relief and freedom from planning legislation. To support the industry in its movement towards greater production, an extension service – the National Agricultural Advisory Services (NAAS), later to become the Agricultural Development and Advisory Service (ADAS) – was created in 1946. Agricultural science was also encouraged, whether in government research stations or in the laboratories of the universities. Membership of the European Economic Community in 1973 did not materially change this planned agriculture. The nature of some state support for farmers changed slightly and decisions influencing farmers' activities came as frequently from Brussels as from Whitehall. But the broad symbiosis between the state (albeit the supra-national state) and the farmers has remained unchanged.

National land use planning in the countryside has parallelled agricultural planning during the twentieth century. Again the 1920s and 1930s and the concern for the effects of the depression provide the main genesis for town and country planning.[7] The key year was again 1947, with the passing of the Town and Country Planning Act which set down the broad structure of development plans, the requirement for permission for development, and the overall objective of safeguarding agricultural land from urban growth. This broad structure has continued to the present time. The key Act is now the Town and Country Planning Act 1971, which replaced the agricultural development plans with a system of general Structure Plans and more detailed Local Plans.[8] But to all intents and purposes, the process of land use planning set up after the Second World War remains.

A second strand of land use planning for the countryside was also created at the end of the Second World War. Pressures for greater access to the open countryside by ordinary people had built up in the 1930s, and with it there had grown a concern to protect special areas which were of high landscape value. These terms came together in the National Parks and Access to the Countryside Act 1949, whereby National Parks and Areas of Outstanding Natural Beauty could be designated, and local authorities were encouraged to facilitate access to the countryside by established rights of way and other methods.[9]

This process of designation led to a substantial proportion of the open countryside being set aside for recreation and access (see below, p. 99). It was not in itself enough, however, to cope with a leisure boom which was perceived in the 1960s. Michael Dower, son of John Dower who had sketched out a scheme of National Parks, graphically represented this movement as the 'fourth wave' of development breaking across the English countryside.[10] The legislative and planning response was the Countryside Act 1968, which transformed the National Parks Commission into a Countryside Commission with responsibility for recreation provision and landscape preservation throughout the countryside and not just within the National Parks.

An urbanized countryside

England's land area, more than any other country in Europe, is still dominated by agricultural uses (table 7.1), despite the frequent alarms sounded by extreme rural preservationists which threaten the imminent covering of rural England under a sea of concrete.

Table 7.1 The land use structure of England and Wales 1901–81

Year	*Population (millions)*	*Agriculture (%)*	*Woodland (%)*	*Urban Land (%)*	*Other Land (%)*
1901	32.5	83.7	5.0	4.5	6.8
1921	37.9	83.1	4.9	5.7	6.3
1931	40.0	82.4	5.6	6.7	5.3
1939	41.5	81.3	6.2	8.0	4.5
1951	43.8	80.5	6.5	8.9	4.1
1961	46.1	79.1	6.9	9.9	4.1
1971	48.8	76.6	7.4	11.0	5.0
1981	49.2	75.2	7.9	11.7	5.2

Source: see note 11

Agriculture still accounts for about three-quarters of the land use of England and Wales or around 11.3 million hectares in about 1981. The decline from the 1901 figures of around 12.6 million hectares for agricultural use is primarily balanced by an increase in urban usage, as will be seen later.

Within the agricultural area there have been very significant changes. The high farming period of the nineteenth century had seen more of England and Wales in cultivation than at any time before or since – more than 6 million hectares of England and Wales were estimated to be in cropland in 1871.[12] Thereafter a massive decline set in and land reverted quickly to scrub and fallow. The Great War expanded cropland areas again as farmers responded to the wartime plough-up campaign and to the promise of stable prices provided by the Corn Production Acts.[13] As already noted, the repeal of this legislation in 1921 heralded a return to permanent grass, rough pasture, and scrub, such that by 1938 there were but 3.6 million hectares in arable cultivation.

The Second World War saw a repeat of the First in so far as the need to increase home food production led to a rapid rise in the arable area.[14] By 1944 the figure for cropland had risen to 5.9 million hectares. While this figure naturally fell slightly in the immediate wartime period as trading links, particularly with North America and the Commonwealth, were re-established, the support given to agriculture by the 1947 Act and subsequent legislation means that the area of land under crops has been maintained at a high level. In 1971 more than 5.6 million hectares were recorded, while 1981 showed a slight drop to 5.5 million.

The reciprocal side of these changes in arable cultivation has been in the area under permanent grass. On most farms at the beginning of the century a significant area was given over to grass, which in some areas had not been ploughed since the enclosure period, if ever. In 1901 two out of every five hectares in agriculture were in permanent grass. Eventually it was this which was taken as the reservoir of land for the wartime plough-up campaigns, with the result that by the 1980s little more than a quarter of the agricultural area is in permanent grass.[15] An important corollary to this change has been the impact upon the natural flora of the countryside and the loss of habitat. Not only have areas passed into cultivation where pesticides, herbicides, and fertilizers have been used to encourage a monoculture, but even more areas left in long-term grassland have often been 'improved' by the selective use of chemicals so that their natural ecological diversity has been destroyed.[16]

England and Wales still have a smaller proportion of their land area under forest and woodland than virtually any other European country. However, the twentieth century has seen a significant increase in the forested area. Barely 5 per cent of the land area (750,000 ha) was forested in 1900, but by the 1980s that figure had grown to nearly 8 per cent (1.2 million ha). In part this has been due to the activities of the Forestry Commission, the state agency formed in 1919 with the specific intention of increasing the forested area. However, the activities of the Commission have generally been concentrated in the upland areas of Wales and especially Scotland. Accordingly a greater role in England can be seen for private forestry interests, albeit encouraged and advised by the Forestry Commission, and by a fiscal system which has tried to increase private afforestation.

Table 7.1 indicates that, despite the continuing domination of agricultural land uses, the urban area of England and Wales has more than doubled since 1900. It has been estimated that in 1901 some 674,000 hectares were in urban and industrial use, while by 1981 that figure had risen to 1.76 million hectares.[17] The increase has thus been substantial, and proportionately much more than the gain in the national population. This last contrast is primarily a function of improvements in urban space standards, reflecting a rejection of the crowded living conditions which had developed in the eighteenth and nineteenth centuries. To some extent, therefore, it indicates a move towards planned development, and especially a tendency to move people out of crowded inner city areas and to re-establish them at lower densities on 'green field' sites. The urbanization of the countryside has been the source of continual debate, particularly since the end of the Second World War. The loss of agricultural land was seen as a major threat to national food production and the ability of the nation to feed itself. In the political sphere this position was ably prosecuted by the National Farmers' Union and it acted as a major bolster to the case for agricultural support. In the broader arena it has frequently been the rallying cry of some extreme agricultural fundamentalist views.[18]

The need to contain the spread of urban Britain, essentially to protect farmland for food production, has been a major contributor to the growth of town and country planning, as has already been outlined.[19] In this regard, fears for the urbanization of the countryside pre-date the Second World War. The 1930s recorded the greatest annual losses of land to urban uses and the result was plain to see. Major urban areas spread out along arterial highways as more than 25,000 hectares of land were built on each year. While town planning legislation had existed in some form since the early years of the century, it was powerless to stop the spread of housing in a situation where agricultural land could be bought cheaply and growing personal mobility allowed the increasing separation of home from work for more and more of the employed population.

At the risk of over-simplification, the twentieth-century growth of the urban area can be divided into four types: ribbon development, suburbanization, town expansion, and planned new settlements. The first was seen especially in the westward spread of London along the Great West Road, and led to the passing of legislation in 1935 in a panicky attempt to stop its ravages. Probably more than any other feature of the urbanization of England, it was seen as a blighting influence upon the countryside and an overwhelming argument for land use planning.

Sururbanization was the rather more ordered expansion of major towns and cities whereby large areas of land on the urban fringe passed into built-up use. By the outbreak of the Second World War it was estimated that half the population was housed in urban areas which had grown since the turn of the century. The expansion of London into the home counties, and especially to the north and west to form what became known as 'Metroland', is the classic case.

In terms of visible result there was little to distinguish this growth of suburbia from town expansion. Small market towns which showed themselves to be increasingly accessible to the major cities had grown especially during the 1930s. The result, by wartime, was viewed by some with horror – hence Betjeman's injunction 'Come, friendly bombs and fall on Slough'. Not only was the loss of farmland deplored, but scorn was poured upon the uniformity of development and the attempt to create character and style, shown quintessentially in the so-called 'Tudorbethan' half-timbering of housing fronting the new highways. After the Second World War the increasing involvement of the state ensured that town growth took on a more formalized pattern. Under the Town Development Act of 1952 individual towns were encouraged to make agreements with London for the transfer of people from inner-urban areas to new housing built out into the countryside.

Planned new settlements, often on green field sites in the open countryside, have been a particular feature of urbanization in England and Wales. The origins of new towns are conventionally seen in the ideas of Ebenezer Howard, and especially in his seminal book *Garden Cities for Tomorrow* (1902), originally published in 1898 as *Tomorrow: A Peaceful Path to Real Reform*; but, as Gillian Darley has shown, the new settlement in the countryside has a much older pedigree.[20] While Letchworth was developed as the first Garden City from 1903, and Welwyn Garden City from 1920, the heyday of new town development came with state patronage after the Second World War. The New Towns Act of 1946, preceded by a Royal Commission under Sir John Reith, provided the original foundation for the creation of more than twenty new settlements. While some were entirely new creations, many were major additions to existing settlements.

The acceptable aspect of the twentieth-century urbanization of the countryside has revolved around an improvement in living conditions for the working population. From the post-First World War demands for 'homes fit for heroes' to the later developments of suburbia and new towns, the assumption has been that urban encroachment has been for housing. The place of industry in the countryside has been much more problematical. Even more than housing, industry has been seen by many as having its proper place in the existing towns and cities. This attitude was perhaps most clearly enunciated in the *Report of the Committee on Land Utilisation in Rural Areas*,[21] under Lord Justice Scott, where, despite a minority report by Professor Dennison, the clear preference for agriculture as the dominant industry in the countryside was shown.

The inter-war period, in fact, had shown significant growth in industry in the countryside, particularly those areas which were accessible to towns. A survey in the early 1930s showed that almost half the industries which had been established to the north-west of London since 1914 had migrated from London itself.[22] They were attracted there, as were entirely new firms, by cheaper land values, the availability of space for expansion and the ease of transportation by road. Such movements were epitomized by the building of the Hoover factory out of London on the Great West Road, and the siting of a new factory for the chemical conglomerate, ICI, in Welwyn Garden City.

As with housing development, the inter-war spread of industries out of towns to green field sites continued apace after the Second World War. Even in the 1930s it had been realized that the south-east of England was proving especially attractive, not only to commuters, but increasingly to 'footloose' industries who were often attracted from the old industrial areas of the urban north. The growth of industries employing new technological developments such as electronics added another factor. The end result has been a continuing concern for the 'overheating' of the economy of the south-east of England and the consequent decline of the north. More specifically, industries have been attracted to the countryside away from urban centres, including London. For new industrialists the attractions of the countryside are many: space to develop factory premises, a clean and attractive working and residential environment for employees, easy access to markets provided by a motorway network, and possible freedom from established union-tied labour forces.[23]

It is now realized that contrary to all expectations, a major dynamic element in the industrial structure of England and Wales has been the nature of the countryside itself. Judged by employment change, the region which has shown by far the largest growth trend since the 1950s has been East Anglia, followed by the south-west of England. While manufacturing industry has generally declined overall and has been replaced in employment terms by the service industries, the growth in manufacturing which has taken place has been disproportionately greater in the more rural areas, and especially in small towns in the countryside.[24] The service industries which have grown have also often chosen rural locations. Overall the position has been that in times of economic depression rurally-located industries have tended to suffer less than their urban counterparts; in times of economic growth they have often surged ahead.

One final important change has happened during the twentieth century with regard to land use change – the increased use of the countryside for purposes of amenity, conservation, and recreation. All three may be seen as further examples of an increasing urban orientation to the use of the countryside. Indeed the designation of areas of countryside for these purposes, which has already been outlined, was essentially the result of pressure from urban people which had developed especially during the 1920s and 1930s. In excess of 20 per cent of the land area of England and Wales is now covered by some form of broad conservation/amenity designation. Some of this land is available to the urban public in so far as it has been specifically set aside for recreation and access as a major use. These areas include country parks, set up following the Countryside Act of 1968, some areas of common land and conservation reserves, and other areas of public and private open space. But a majority of the 1.2 million hectares which one authority[25] estimated as 'land available for public recreation', are in some form of multiple use, usually agriculture. While the general public is often uncertain of its right of access over private farmland, it has become more and more aware of the complex network of footpaths in the countryside. One estimate has put the total length of footpaths in England and Wales at more than 190,000 kilometres.[26] While some county councils have been laggard in registering these resources, public effort, often backed up by the pressure of the Ramblers' Association and local footpath groups, have opened up many old pathways to general recreational use. Land for recreational use overlaps to a significant extent with land which is used for nature conservation purposes.[27] Some of this land exists as statutory National Nature Reserves, owned by the Nature Conservancy Council or, more commonly, leased from or used by agreement with private landowners. A major force in this area has been county naturalist trusts, which are voluntary organizations committed to nature conservation, and which own substantial areas of land in their own right.

Conclusion

The use of the countryside for recreation and nature conservation by a largely urban population has been a major theme in the development of the English countryside in the second half of the twentieth century. But this is just one component, albeit an important one, in the gradual adoption of the countryside, its images and its resources, by a significant proportion of the urban population. Until the Second World War it is fair to argue that concern and interest regarding the countryside was very much the preserve of the middle and upper classes. It was really only from among these numerically small groups that people could be found who owned or used rural land or who were concerned about its appearance. In the post-war years, however, the countryside has become the property of a large majority of the population. Rising personal incomes, the availability of private transport, the growth in paid holidays and leisure time – all these have been factors to encourage the urban public to feel a proprietorial interest in the countryside.

The indications of this interest are many. The membership of 'countryside' societies is one: around one in fifty of the entire population is a registered member of the National Trust; the Royal Society for the Protection of Birds had nearly 400,000 members in the mid 1980s; studies by the Countryside Commission estimate that many millions of urban people visit the countryside for recreation and leisure. The house in the country (and even more so the second home) has again become the ultimate status symbol. More subtly, the image of the English countryside pervades urban lifestyles every day.[28] Manufacturers (and even more their advertising agencies) have seized upon rural and countryside themes to sell everything from foodstuffs to clothing, secure in the knowledge that consumers will warm to the association of their product with qualities of naturalness, health, and value.

Of course, this urban take-over of the countryside has involved and affected the rural dwellers themselves. No longer are those who live in the countryside considered a race apart as their attitudes and mores, their lifestyles and their aspirations, have become increasingly entwined with those of the town dwellers. It is this change which will be addressed in the following chapter.

Notes

1 Williams, 1973.
2 Rogers, Blunden, and Curry, 1985.
3 This viewpoint has perhaps been most earnestly argued by Shoard, 1980.
4 Ministry of Works and Planning, 1942.
5 This view has been put by Coleman, 1976, 411–37.
6 The progress of agricultural depression was not of course even, and within the period there were times of comparative improvement, if not prosperity. For a critical analysis of the period, see Perry, 1974.
7 The origins of town and country planning and of the growing role of the land use planner are discussed in G. E. Cherry's official history of the Royal Town Planning Institute (Cherry, 1974). See also vol. 1 of the official peacetime history of environmental planning (Cullingworth, 1975).
8 Cullingworth, 1985.
9 Cherry, 1975 (vol. 2 of the official peacetime history of environmental planning), provides what is probably the most detailed account of the growth of the 'access movement' in the pre-war period. As well as published sources, it makes use of unpublished cabinet minutes and other official reports. A more polemical account of the movement to create National Parks (and of their subsequent development) can be found in McEwen and McEwen, 1987.
10 John Dower's report on *National Parks in England and Wales* (Cmnd 6628) was published in 1945 and was used as the basis for discussions on the creation of a National Park system in England and Wales. Twenty years later his son, Michael, was the author of a report for the Civic Trust, *Fourth Wave: the Challenge of Leisure*, 1965, which was influential in forming opinion and presaged the 'leisure boom' of the late 1960s.
11 Best, 1981; Best and Anderson, 1984, 21–4.
12 Coppock, 1962.
13 Sheail, 1981.
14 The eminent agricultural economist, Edith Whetham, quotes an increase in the area under tillage from 3,604,000 ha in 1936–8 to 5,212,000 ha in 1947 (Whetham, 1952).

15 Best and Anderson, 1984.
16 Green, 1985.
17 Best, 1981.
18 For examples of this perspective, see Coleman, 1976; Moss, 1976.
19 The classic account of the success of post-war British planning in preventing the spread of towns can be found in Hall, Thomas, Gracey, and Drewett, 1973.
20 Darley, 1975.
21 Ministry of Works and Planning, 1942.
22 Smith, 1933.
23 Fothergill and Gudgin, 1982.
24 See, for example, Keeble and Gould, 1985.
25 Burton and Wibberley, 1965.
26 Patmore, 1983.
27 Green, 1985.
28 McLaughlin, 1986a.

8

People in the countryside

Alan Rogers

The process of twentieth-century urbanization which was considered in the previous chapter has been much more than a matter of land use change and the physical spread of the built-up area. Of much greater significance has been the 'urbanization of the mind', that is, the revolution in the attitudes and activities of those who live and work in the countryside. Urban land uses have been seen to have covered only a relatively minor part of the land surface, leaving well over 80 per cent of England to rural use. While more difficult to measure, there has been a much more complete spread of urban mores and behaviour patterns into the countryside.

The farm worker, living with his family in the tied cottage in the depths of the Devon countryside, may superficially appear to be very similar in circumstance to his grandfather who inhabited the same cottage eighty years before. On closer inspection, however, the situation is seen to be very different. His wages are still low, relative to his more affluent neighbours, but they are spent on packaged foodstuffs and consumer goods which are the same as those bought by the residents of the big cities. Both he and his family have experienced an educational system which is common to the rest of the nation and which rarely makes reference to their immediate local rural circumstances. Each evening the family participate in world events as international news and entertainment from other nations appear on the television screen. It is possible that one or more of his children will follow him on to the farm, but it is more likely that they will leave for the nearby town or for the city in the search for employment.

This aspect of urbanization can be exaggerated, of course. Many of the old structures of village life are intact, even thriving. The public house, the village hall, the flower show are all well supported. The participants, however, are not just the descendants of the nineteenth-century village. They are joined by the office-working commuter, the retired professional man and his wife, and (if only at weekends and in the summer) by the second homer.

Life in the lowland English village of the late twentieth century has arguably not seen such buoyancy, or indeed prosperity, since Thomas Hardy detailed rural life in the Wessex of a hundred years earlier. Yet paradoxically there exists the general view that village life has been destroyed, and 'loss of community' is a common cry. By contrast, countless authors, both of fact and fiction, look backwards to tell the tale of the apparently thriving village life of long ago, indulging in what the sociologist Howard Newby has perceptively called 'rural retrospective regret'.[1]

A middle-class countryside

In the middle of the Second World War, when some minds were beginning to turn to thoughts of rural reconstruction, the eminent agricultural economist Charles Stuart Orwin conducted a survey of an area of rural north Oxfordshire. His objective was to set out the range of problems which would face a typical rural area when peace returned, and which would need to be addressed by public policy. The book which resulted, though long out of print, remains one of the classics of twentieth-century rural research.[2]

While Orwin was broad and comprehensive in his survey, his analysis centred on two major problems facing the countryside of the 1940s. One was the continued loss of people which had been going on everywhere since the 1870s and 1880s (and since before mid-century in some areas) and had reached the point where villages were often barely half the size that they had been sixty years before. Houses lay derelict and the young and dynamic element of the population had long since moved to the town. The second was the condition of the farming industry, battered by years of depression and competition from cheap imports, unable to provide a decent livelihood for farmers and farmworkers alike, and yet contributing barely 40 per cent of the national food supply.

Orwin was a perceptive man and one capable of more foresight and imagination than most. He saw the future for the rural areas in terms of the modernization of agriculture, with the resulting increase in productivity leading to a more prosperous countryside, higher levels of home production, and a halt to population loss in the villages. The two major problems of agricultural depression and rural depopulation were inextricably linked. In the years since his death in 1955 the population of rural England has grown very substantially and the countryside now produces virtually all the temperate foodstuffs which the nation needs, yet the number of those employed in agriculture has declined to barely one-fifth of its 1955 total. The countryside may be more prosperous and farming has certainly been revolutionized, but this has not been achieved by keeping people on the land.

Throughout most of the nineteenth century, while the national population grew fourfold, population in the rural areas remained static.[3] By 1851 the rural population made up less than one half of the national total. The process of out-migration from the countryside, exacerbated at times by low birth rates, continued into the present century to the point where, at the outbreak of the Second World War, less than one person in five lived in a rural area.[4] The process of relative population decline was not, of course uniform, and in the inter-war period rural populations generally continued to remain static. None the less, over a hundred years of stagnation and relative decline were enough to convince most authorities that the 'drift from the land' was the root cause of most rural ills.

The slackening of depopulation trends in the inter-war period should have given a hint that the tide of rural population was on the change. The extension of people and houses into the suburbs which was noted in chapter 7 was an indication of the future pattern. Already by the 1930s the more accessible villages and small towns were growing as the new arterial roads and the railway system allowed more and more people to divorce their rural home from their urban workplace.[5] After the Second World War the process continued but at a greater pace. The distances over which people were able, and willing, to travel grew as a motorway network and a speedier intercity train service were put in place.

Of major significance in this process was the growth in the private ownership of the motor car, which in England grew from little more than 2 million vehicles in 1950 to more than 16 million in 1985. Indeed it is by no means an exaggeration to consider the motor car as the single most significant development in the process of countryside change in the twentieth century. Not only has it been the major agent in allowing the spread of suburbs and the growth of commuting, but it also made possible the re-population of the countryside on a permanent basis. Moreover, it has been the key factor in the 'leisure explosion' and the use of the countryside for informal recreation. Within the village and the market town the ownership – and more particularly the lack of ownership – of a motor car presents one of the clearest indications of social differentiation amongst rural households.

In total contrast to the demographic changes of the previous century the population of the countryside since the middle of the present century has grown substantially. The process of re-population has parallels in all other western countries, and it is now seen as a natural stage of economic development which occurs as countries move towards the very end of the demographic transition and into a 'post-industrial' world.[6] At an early stage the process in the United States was termed 'counter-urbanization' or the 'population turnaround'. While the major urban centres, and especially the big conurbations, have lost population, the countryside areas have gained. Between 1961 and 1971 Greater London lost 6.8 per cent of its population; a further 10.1 per cent drop was recorded between 1971 and 1981.[7] A similar order of loss was recorded in the other metropolitan districts. In contrast, small towns and villages grew in population. Between 1961 and 1971 growth averaged around 8 per cent at a time when national population totals increased by no more than 0.5 per cent. Perhaps even more surprisingly, the remote, less accessible rural districts also grew by around 10 per cent in each decade.

This population turnaround has had a profound influence upon the state of the English countryside. In terms simply of numbers it has meant more populous villages and small towns. But the social impact of this trend has been of greater significance because counter-urbanization has introduced not just more people into the countryside but different people. In other words not only has there been an importation of largely urban attitudes through the medium of newspapers, television, a common educational system, and the like, but also through the invasion of urban people themselves.

An early field study of this process was carried out in north Hertfordshire by the sociologist, Ray Pahl.[8] In what is now regarded as a classic study, he pointed to the differences of attitude and behaviour between old and new residents and the resulting community tension which arose within the community. In a further study he sketched out a new typology of social structure for lowland rural England, which is still a valuable checklist in understanding these social changes (table 8.1).[9]

Table 8.1 Pahl's Typology of the English Village

1	large property owners
2	salaried immigrants with some capital
3	'spiralists'
4	those with limited income and little capital
5	the retired
6	council house tenants
7	tied cottagers and other tenants
8	local tradesmen and owners of small businesses

Source: see note 9

It will be clear that this classification is a mixture of both old and new village populations. Some, such as the large property owners, have always been there. Others are quite new, especially the salaried immigrants and their generally younger and more transient colleagues, the so-called 'spiralists' (executive households). Yet others have changed in some way as with the private tenants who have often been replaced by the local authority tenants.

The important feature to realize about this typology is its significance for understanding the changing political economy of rural areas and, in particular, the differential needs and competitive positions of groups in rural society. As Pahl said, 'There is no village population as such: rather there are specific populations which for various, but identifiable, reasons find themselves in a village.'[10] These specific populations have different needs, different income levels, and above all, different aspirations, prejudices, and ideals. They may have very different ideas of what the countryside and 'their' village means for them, and these different ideas may well clash with the ideas of other groups. In such clashes are the seeds of important conflicts within the present-day English village community.

Class conflict in the nineteenth century was essentially predicated upon the classic social and economic disposition of master and man. The conflict between farmers and landowners as the owners and controllers of capital and the farmworkers who had only their labour, led to continual tension, albeit often under a cloak of benevolent patronage, and gave rise to some classic confrontations. The most famous of the latter was, of course, the saga of the Tolpuddle Martyrs. In the present century, this conflict has been replaced by a much broader-based set of tensions between several groups. Moreover, while the previous conflict was between two classes which were both involved with farming, this later clash is between groups both in and out of agriculture. Howard Newby has described this change as one from an 'occupational community', centred on the dominant industry of agriculture, to an 'encapsulated community'.[11] By this he means that the farming groups, both farmers and workers, have found themselves very much reduced in numbers and effectively surrounded by other social groupings which have little or no interest or knowledge of agriculture. The labour tensions of the past have been replaced by new tensions within the village which have come about as a direct result of a clash between two views of the countryside.

Two examples will make this point clear. For commuters and retired settlers from the urban area, a major attraction of moving to the countryside is the opportunity to live in an attractive house, often with land attached. To gain such a foothold they have been prepared to pay high prices for rural property and have easily been able to outbid local people who cannot compete in the housing market, not least because of the generally lower level of rural wages.[12] A major source of tension over housing competition has thus arisen. Further tension arises when 'incomers' feel that their particular bit of the countryside is threatened, especially if the threat comes from the local farming community. This problem is most clearly seen in issues such as hedgerow removal, straw burning, or the noise of agricultural machinery. Modern agricultural techniques often do not square with the incomers' view of the countryside, based upon a vague and dated myth. These new social groupings in the countryside have another characteristic which makes their presence important. They are often vocal, articulate, and very able to do something to forward their viewpoint. They have been largely responsible for the rapid growth in the number of pressure groups in rural areas which have often grown up as a reaction to a perceived threat to a cherished environment. This theme is explored in more detail in the final chapter in this book by Philip Lowe.

The position of farmers and farmworkers within the social structure of the English village has altered radically in the wake of these demographic and social changes. The farmer still has social standing within the community, but he finds himself in company with the retired bank manager and the commuting executive on the parish council and the village hall committee. No longer is his view taken as law, and he may be challenged and argued with as never in the past. Even more pertinent may be the fact that his income level no longer automatically puts him ahead of all others in the village.

For the farmworker the position has also changed. The income differentials will have been exacerbated as he finds himself earning not only much less than his employer, but less than his urban-employed neighbour. His position has also altered as the numbers of farmworkers have declined and his feeling of isolation, as well as material deprivation, has increased. Behind the prosperous façade of the English countryside in the last decades of the century there can be found a level of deprivation which is surprising, not to say embarrassing. For all the prosperity of farming in the forty years since the 1947 Agriculture Act, wages in the agricultural industry have consistently remained at no more than two-thirds of the level of other manual jobs. A government-sponsored study into rural deprivation in the early 1980s suggested that around one household in every five in rural areas was living at or below the poverty line.[13] Moreover, the existence in many rural areas of incomers employed in non-manual occupations which are significantly above national (let alone rural) averages simply exacerbates the poverty issue. The gaps between rich and poor which were evident in the Victorian village are still to be found. The only thing to have changed is that the rich minority has often become a majority, with a sizeable minority which may arguably be relatively even more disadvantaged than before.

A countryside for leisure

While the residential population of rural areas has increased, there has been another major invasion of urban people into the countryside. On an average Sunday in the summer the resident population is effectively doubled as 15 million urban people visit the countryside for leisure purposes. This is the 'Fourth Wave' which was referred to in the previous chapter – the surge of people out from the towns intent on spending some hours of relaxation in the countryside.[14] Mass movements of urban people for recreational purposes go back to the 1840s with the advent of the 'day trip' to the seaside resorts provided for by the railway companies. These grew in popularity as incomes rose and as ordinary working people gained more holidays and free time. But these railway trips largely bypassed the countryside, which was not seen as a recreation resource. The key to the opening up of the countryside for leisure purposes was, as has already been mentioned, the motor car.

Private motoring grew in the inter-war period, but it remained the prerogative of the well-off middle class. It was not until the 1950s that the private motor car became a possibility for many ordinary families. By the following decade the combination of rising incomes, shorter working hours, and the availability of mass-produced cars had set the scene for an explosion in leisure. The coastal resort and the open coast have to some extent retained their popularity as a destination for leisure trips, but mainly when people have the time, measured in days rather than hours, to devote to holidays rather than shorter informal day trips. For day excursions it is the countryside which has come into its own. Some are prepared to travel significant distances, for example to view historic houses or visit specific sites where facilities for recreation may be provided. For many others, however, no special provision is required – the actual activity of driving gently along country lanes is all that is needed. While both local authorities and private entrepreneurs have increasingly provided services and facilities to enhance the 'recreation experience', these are superfluous for many visitors. For them their essential recreational needs can be summed up in the catch-phrase 'the brew, the loo, and the view'. Early on in the development of this outdoor recreation trend researchers recognized the significance of the motor car, not only as a means of transportation but as part of recreation itself. Indeed one authority argued that the car is in effect a 'room on wheels', part of the urban home which can be taken into the countryside and which allows the occupants to experience a moderated introduction to the countryside rather than the 'raw' real nature of rural areas.[15]

In response to this massive growth in the use of the countryside, there has grown up a veritable recreation industry. Some of this is sponsored by the public sector; local authorities, in particular, have provided country parks and picnic sites, tourist information points and guided walks. Other public authorities, for example the Forestry Commission, have also contributed. The private sector has responded by the provision of sites and facilities, some on a grand scale such as Disney-type theme parks, others more commonly on a small scale as with individual enterprises on farms.

For much of the early growth period in the 1960s and 1970s, this recreation boom was seen as peripheral and irrelevant to the main land-using activity in the countryside, farming. True it was recognized that some small farms, for example in the south-west of England, had for a long time added to their income by providing bed and breakfast and other related services. Indeed, in the early 1970s it was officially estimated that recreation activities earned English farmers at least £50 million each year.[16] But for most mainstream farmers, the introduction of recreation enterprises into their farm business was seen as demeaning and an admission of business failure in their 'proper' activities. The decline in farm incomes and the call for diversification to combat the problems of surplus food production and the high cost of budgetary support, have radically changed this view. Recreation enterprises on farms are now positively encouraged as one possible solution to an economic crisis.[17] This can only mean that Dower's Fourth Wave is still breaking and the countryside will more and more become an urban playground as well as a food factory.

For a minority of urban people the countryside has provided a very particular form of recreation in the form of the second home. At the end of the 1960s it was widely believed that Britain would follow many other countries in western Europe, notably in France and in Scandinavia, and see a growth in the ownership of 'country cottages' to the point where, perhaps by the end of the century, around 30 or 40 per cent of all households would have access to a second home. An officially-sponsored survey at that time suggested that there were perhaps around 300,000 such properties, with an annual growth rate of perhaps 25,000 per year.[18] This growth rate was certainly not maintained in the 1970s as economic depression grew, and it seems likely that no more than 500,000 second homes now exist. In fact this can be explained by a laggard economy, but there are at least two other more basic reasons. First, the English countryside generally lacks that great wealth of rural houses which are characteristic of large parts of western Europe and which reflect a countryside which until very recently was populous and full of farmers. The migration of people into the towns and the villages effectively took with it the housing which they occupied. Secondly, the strict planning regulations (see chapter 7) which came into effect after 1947 have largely prevented the building of purpose-made holiday homes.

This is not to say, however, that second homes do not present a problem in particular localities. In some especially attractive rural areas, such as the National Parks, they are very common and it is not unusual to find some villages where half the housing stock is in periodic holiday use. This causes local resentment as country people find it impossible to purchase permanent homes when they are out-priced by urban dwellers who thus add to the local housing pressures noted earlier in this chapter. In some areas, there is concern at the temporary but persistent invasion of non-locals which leaves the villages empty for large parts of the year and which threaten local culture and, in the special case of Wales, local language.[19] In this last case, resentment has occasionally grown into direct action as second homes have been burned and destroyed in protest.

The rural idyll: end or beginning?

This chapter has concentrated upon tracing some important elements of human change in the English countryside during the twentieth century. The themes which have come through are those of growth and dynamism, of invasions of people, and of critical social conflicts. For some these changes have apparently brought an end to what they perceive to have been a rural idyll. The destruction of a local economy and a local society founded upon agriculture and the destruction of a much-loved landscape by modern farming practice have conspired to destroy the image of the English countryside which is so carefully preserved in literature and art. For some it may be possible to re-create a version of this good life through the country retreat – but as the number of people aspiring to this goal increases, the attainment of it becomes less precious. In this way rural living has been designated as a 'positional good' by Fred Hirsch – that is, something which is given a value above its obvious material worth simply because it remains accessible to relatively few people.[20] As more and more people move to the countryside then that exclusiveness which is the rural idyll gradually disappears. Moreover, a distinctively rural way of life becomes progressively changed as urban ideas take over.

This essentially pessimistic view – Newby's 'rural retrospective regret' carried to an extreme and depressing conclusion – is, however, but one perspective. It is equally possible to argue the alternative case: that distinctive rural lifestyles are still to be found, though different in character from their nineteenth-century equivalents. Moreover it is this perceived distinctiveness which has proved the major engine of the processes of counter-urbanization and leisure growth which have been traced in this chapter. To many millions of urban-based people it acts as a powerful magnet which attracts them to the countryside to live, to relax, and increasingly, to work. Social exclusiveness is not a necessary part of their rural idyll. Some have even suggested that the re-population of the countryside will eventually give rise to a nation of small communities, linked nationally and internationally by advanced electronic methods of communication but re-creating the local, small-scale community structures of the village of the past.[21] In this view the village becomes both the geographical and the social unit of the future and the rural idyll: far from being destroyed by the developments of the century, it becomes the property of the masses.

Notes

1 A classic analysis of social change in the countryside, at least as observed in lowland England, is to be found in Newby, 1979.

2 The survey was published in 1944 as *Country Planning; a Study of Rural Problems*, under the collective authorship of the Oxford Agricultural

Economics Research Institute, Oxford, Oxford University Press. Subsequently in 1946 the Central Office of Information produced a film entitled *Twenty Four Square Miles*, which was based closely on the survey, and was intended, as was the original, to set out an agenda for rural reconstruction. A video copy of the film is now available from Trilith Video, Corner Cottage, Brickyard Lane, Bourton, near Gillingham, Dorset.
3 Lawton, 1973.
4 The classic account of this process has been given in Saville, 1957.
5 J. T. Coppock has provided an interesting illustration of this process in the case of Radlett in Hertfordshire. See Coppock and Prince, 1964.
6 See Vining and Kontuly, 1978, 49–73. One leading authority, Peter Hall, has called this movement 'The Industrial Revolution in reverse': see Hall, 1988, 15–19.
7 Champion, 1981.
8 Pahl, 1965.
9 Pahl, 1966, 1146–50.
10 ibid.
11 Newby, 1979.
12 For a review of the arguments on 'local housing need', see Rogers, 1985, 367–80.
13 McLaughlin, 1986b, 291–307. For a broader and more comprehensive assessment of this contemporary issue, see Lowe, Bradley, and Wright, 1986.
14 Dower, 1965. The publications of the Countryside Commission, the government agency charged with policy for recreation, provide further evidence of the nature of the leisure boom. For an authoritative and very readable academic assessment, see Patmore, 1983.
15 This view was put forward by Burton, 1967.
16 Countryside Commission, 1974.
17 In early 1987 the government issued a broad policy document under the general heading of *Farming and Rural Enterprise*, London, HMSO. Recreation and tourism enterprises were given significant emphasis.
18 Bielckus, Rogers, and Wibberley, 1972.
19 For a good, though now rather dated review of these issues, see Coppock, 1977.
20 Hirsch, 1977.
21 See, for example, Smigelski, 1978.

9

The rural idyll defended: from preservation to conservation

Philip Lowe

The nineteenth-century roots of rural preservation

In his exhaustive account of changing attitudes to the natural world in Britain between 1500 and 1800, Keith Thomas reveals a temporal progression of attitudes and behaviour to nature such that, by the end of the period, the characteristic attitude is no longer 'one of exaltation in hard-won human dominance'.[1] Ascendancy over the natural world may have remained the aim of most people in practice, but it was no longer an unquestioned objective. Indeed, 'there had gradually emerged attitudes to the natural world which were essentially incompatible with the direction in which English society was moving'.[2] Towns created a longing for the countryside; cultivation, for unsubdued nature; new-found security from wild animals, for species protection. Thus it was increasingly hard for society to come to terms with the ruthless methods upon which its material comfort depended, and Thomas identifies this as one of the contradictions on which modern civilization rests.

Since the late eighteenth century and the experience of successive waves of industrialism these concerns and anxieties have become heightened. Indeed, right from its earliest stages, industrialization has provoked popular reactions which have been partly nostalgic for the disappearing, pre-industrial world; partly apocalyptic, fearing the outcome of the Faustian bargain of technological society; and partly utopian in seeking to re-create community and human solidarity out of the dislocation and fragmentation wrought by industrialism. During the nineteenth century many of these concerns and values found expression in various social movements.[3]

A number of pressure groups and voluntary organizations, formed in the late nineteenth and early twentieth centuries to preserve wildlife, landscape, open spaces, and antiquities, established the roots of the contemporary environmental movement, including the following groups:

Society for Checking the Abuses of Public Advertising	1863
Commons Preservation Society (now the Open Spaces Society)	1865
Society for the Protection of Ancient Buildings	1877
National Footpaths Preservation Society	1884
Selbourne Society for the Protection of Birds, Plants and Pleasant Places	1885
Society for the Protection of Birds (now the Royal Society for the Protection of Birds)	1889
National Trust for Places of Historic Interest and Natural Beauty	1894
Society for the Preservation of the Wild Fauna of the Empire (now the Fauna & Flora Preservation Society)	1903
British Empire Naturalists' Association (now the British Naturalists' Association)	1905
Society for the Promotion of Nature Reserves (now the Royal Society for Nature Conservation)	1912

This preservationist concern was an integral part of the late Victorian intellectual reaction to many of the tenets of economic liberalism, including a reversal of the rationalist, progressivist outlook deriving from the Enlightenment which, with its confidence in the perfectibility of all things, had looked always to the improvement of nature and society through the exercise of human reason. It is no coincidence, for example, that some of the social philosophers and writers in the vanguard of this reaction, such as John Stuart Mill, John Ruskin, William Morris, Thomas Huxley, Lord Avebury, and William Henry Hudson, were founder members of preservationist groups. This profound shift of opinion, with its rejection of the imperative to improve, arose from a reassessment of the social and economic changes of the nineteenth century, fuelled by moral and aesthetic reaction to the urban condition.

During the nineteenth century Britain had been transformed from an economy based on agriculture to one based on industry and commerce. Between 1801 and 1911 the proportion of the population living in urban areas rose from 20 per cent to 80 per cent. In the burgeoning industrial cities, with their jerry-built terraces and tenements wedged between smoky factories, mills, and foundries, working and living conditions were cramped, polluted, and insanitary. Trade fluctuations led to recurrent unemployment, and in the larger centres, with their multitude of sweat shops and large reserves of casual labour, abject poverty and destitution were commonplace.

After the mid century, as the demands on public and charitable relief increased, as the early social surveys revealed the extent of the suffering, and as fear of the mob intensified, so middle-class opinion was increasingly disturbed by urban conditions and the predicament of the urban poor. In art and literature, Victorian prosperity and respectability came to be depicted as a façade barely concealing an inferno of verminous activity, the poor preying on each other and the rich smug in their complacency and hypocrisy. The optimism and belief in boundless prosperity that had characterized the early Victorian period was displaced by pessimism about the prospects for social and economic advance.

The Victorians' self-confidence was sapped by the Great Depression of the 1880s and by the intellectual crisis of the post-Darwinian years which cast doubt on the nature of the human condition and the possibility of its improvement.[4] Britain's increasingly disappointing industrial performance in the final decades of the century was matched by a growing equivocation towards industrialism itself: the source of the nation's economic and political power was coming to be seen as destructive of the moral and social order, human health, traditional values, the physical environment, and natural beauty. This growing antipathy to the industrial spirit in late nineteenth-century Britain reflected the absorption of the urban bourgeoisie into the upper reaches of British society and its genteel value system – a value system which disdained trade and industry, which stressed civilized enjoyment, rather than accumulation of wealth, and which preferred social stability to enterprise.[5]

Anti-industrial values infected social criticism and were embodied in various institutions and campaigns that sought to preserve facets of traditional society and culture from the ravages of urban growth. The countryside, in particular, became the object of both veneration and concern. In the words of one historian:

> In the iconography of the age, the city stood for misery and ugliness, the countryside for bliss and beauty. As the countryside became the source of all that was divine, so the city was seen as infernal, with all the potent imagery associated with hell.[6]

In literature, the countryside was idealized as the setting for traditional and harmonious social relations.[7] The poetry of the period, drawing on romanticism and classical pantheism, presented love of Nature as a transcendental experience, a form of worship; a mystical attachment to Nature, when faith in a conventional creator was on the wane, seemed to feed people's unquenched spiritual needs in an increasingly godless and materialistic age.

The symbolic importance of the countryside grew as its economic and social importance were eclipsed. The late 1870s saw the collapse of agriculture as cheap food, transported by railroad and steamship, flooded into Britain from overseas. Much land went out of cultivation. Whereas previously industrial expansion had drawn people off the land, now immiseration and despair drove them into the cities and to emigration. The rural population declined sharply and many village communities sank into depression. The cause of rural preservation was therefore given added poignancy by a sense that the traditional order of the countryside was on the verge of extinction. Antiquarians, artists, folklorists, and photographers sought to document the vanishing rural world, to record and if possible, preserve remnants of country life – traditional customs, regional dialects, village crafts, folk-songs, country dances, rustic lore, and legend – all of which seemed to testify to a former way of life, harder yet happier, simpler, and wiser.[8]

It is easy to present the late nineteenth-century concern for rural preservation as something entirely nostalgic and backward-looking in its attachment to a disappearing (if not mythical) rural world, and as escapist and other-worldly in turning its back on the acute problems of the city. This is the line taken by a number of social critics and historians, who see in rural preservation at best an effete indulgence, at worst a perniciously diverting and debilitating illusion which has nourished reactionary views.[9] Certainly, rural preservationism always did and still does contain elements of nostalgia and romanticism. But such a summary judgement overlooks the importance of the preservation movement in easing the transition from a traditional, rural society to a secular, urban one, and overlooks certain progressive elements within it.

First of all, it seems entirely misconceived to portray anti-urbanism in Victorian Britain as irrational. Most of the industrial towns and cities were foul and insanitary – not just unpleasant, but unhealthy places. Regulations for health, safety, and human exploitation were only gradually established through factory and public health legislation. As the first industrial nation, Britain had to deal with complex and unknown problems. The social and political reaction to industrialism needs to be assessed in a broader, international context. By comparison with the role of anti-industrial ideology in Germany, for example, the integration of these strands of thought within British society should be evaluated more favourably.[10]

Secondly, it is mistaken to label rural preservationism as necessarily escapist. Many of the key figures who pressed for the protection of antiquities, wildlife, and natural beauty were also prominent in campaigns to improve the urban environment – for example, towards better standards of town planning, improved housing conditions, more open spaces, and the control of air pollution. Admittedly, some of these reformers, such as the formidable Octavia Hill, did not challenge the capitalist system, but others, including William Morris, did. Such virtues or failings should not blind us to their tangible achievements in ameliorating urban conditions and in promoting their visions of a more civilized society.

A third, progressive element was the relationship between the preservationist movement and emerging patterns of recreation and leisure, linked to concerns for the physical and mental health of an urbanized population.

Towards the end of the nineteenth century a whole range of outdoor pursuits became fashionable, including rambling, cycling, climbing, camping, caravanning, angling, natural history, and field sports. Their proponents were often preservationists as well as vice versa. These activities offered relief from monotonous routine, and exercise and refreshment for city dwellers, including creative outlets for the leisure opportunities progressively being opened up to ever broader social strata through the growth of real wages, shorter working hours, and the spread of the railways.

The consequences for rural land use were not always progressive, with large tracts of land being turned over to game, for example, and 'the pheasant ousting the peasant'. But the rural preservation movement campaigned vigorously to revive ancient and often practically defunct rights and to re-define these to suit the recreational and health needs of an urban society – for example, the campaigns to preserve suburban commons and to maintain rural footpaths and rights of way. Thereby, the function of rural areas was in part re-defined as an urban amenity. Arguably this was a process that had been going on since the eighteenth century and the creation of landscape parks on the great estates, but now it was being extended to embrace a broader clientele, including, by the turn of the century, the urban middle class, and, by the 1930s, the working class.

The term which came into general currency in the early decades of the twentieth century and signified this new attitude towards rural areas was 'the countryside'. John Betjeman dubbed the word 'a delightful suburbanism [with] a flavour of the garden city about it';[11] and at least initially it did carry the connotations of idyll and repose, as well as of a specific rural prospect beyond the city edge or fleetingly glimpsed through the window of a railway carriage or motor car. Significantly, the fiercest struggles in the re-definition of rural space were not with country people, who remained idealized but neglected, but between the conflicting recreational tastes and means of different urban groups, such as the *battue* of the plutocrats and *nouveaux riches*, the botanizing and rambling of the genteel middle class, and the hiking of the working class. The battles between these groups over rural space were microcosms of their larger struggles for control over the urban social order.

A final, progressive feature of the preservation movement was the faltering steps it made towards an ecological consciousness and an understanding of the need to impose limits on the technological subjugation of the natural world. A crucial factor was a gathering sense of the vulnerability and loss of wildlife, demanding urgent countermeasures. Acceptance of Darwinian evolutionary theory and evidence from the fossil record of extinct animals laid to rest the belief in a God-ordained natural plenitude. *The Origin of Species* presented a different vision – of an uncaring nature, mindlessly murderous, with death and wastage on an enormous scale, whole species formed and then blindly squandered.[12] Equally disturbing was a growing sense of man's own destructive power. A number of species had already been extinguished by over-hunting and human persecution – including the blauwbok, the quagga, the sea mink, the dodo, the Antarctic wolf, the great auk, the marno, the moa, and the passenger pigeon. Many more were threatened, especially the large mammals of Africa, the fur-bearing animals of North America and Siberia, and the colourful birds of the tropics. In Britain, several bird species had become locally extinct, including the osprey, the avocet, the black-tailed godwit, the bustard, and the capercaillie.

It was not simply a matter of the reckless greed of the hunter or the wanton destruction of the sportsman. The causes were more complex and pervasive. The avocet and the black-tailed godwit, for example, were lost during the first half of the nineteenth century, largely due to drainage of their breeding haunts in eastern England. In the words of Charles Rothschild, the founder of the Society for the Promotion of Nature Reserves, 'civilisation and progress are gradually but surely forcing back and destroying the beauties of wild life'.[13] Evidence that many plant species were becoming locally rare or extinct induced the Selborne Society to set up a Plant Protection Section, whose recorder gave the following causes for the decline or extermination of wild plants:

> Smoke; atmospheric abnormalities; drainage; cutting down of woods; desiccation; drought; cultivation; building operations; sport; hawking and collecting; professional collecting; nature-study operations.[14]

The once-stalwart objects of nature now seemed vulnerable and fragile. This was reflected in the changing concept of the balance of nature.[15] In the eighteenth century the term had implied a robust, pre-ordained system of checks and balances which ensured permanency and continuity in nature. By the end of the nineteenth century it conveyed the notion of a delicate and intricate equilibrium, easily disrupted and highly sensitive to human interference. Thus, according to Raphael Meldola, an organic chemist and leading amateur entomologist who led the campaign to retain Epping Forest as a 'biological preserve':[16] 'The workings of nature are connected and bound up in such endless and unsuspected ways that any interference on the part of man may unknowingly upset the adjustments that have taken ages for their perfection.'[17]

Though Darwin had placed man firmly in nature, the Industrial Revolution had irrevocably broken man's bondage to the natural world. Human beings no longer lived in a primitive state. Freed from nature's control, they now saw themselves running amok, wreaking havoc and destruction with a vengeance. The relentless advance of civilization seemed inimical to other living things, and a new image began to emerge of man as a cosmic freak in the evolutionary process. Such awesome power as man increasingly possessed over nature needed to be exercized with proper restraint and care and in full consciousness of the terrible responsibility that man now bore for the fate of the natural world.[18]

The institutional accommodation of rural preservation

Preservation was initially a cause with radical connotations, embracing radical liberals and socialists who challenged what they saw as a philistine and inhuman materialism, as well as absolute notions of property rights and the power of landownership. During the 1870s three successive National Monuments Protection bills were abortively introduced; likewise, in the 1880s, two successive Access to Mountains bills. All were thwarted because of their threatened infringement of private property rights.[19] The connotations changed as compromise measures were sought, and efforts were made to enlist the support of landed and propertied interests. By the turn of the century more conservative forces were at work. Because of their uniqueness, relics of the past and of nature provided a kind of visible guarantee of historical identity, to be preserved from the arbitrary standardization that a cosmopolitan industrialism seemed to threaten.[20] With mounting international tension and a growing concern for internal order and the unity of the kingdom, the past and the countryside were presented as a collective inheritance expressing the essential national spirit; and increasingly these images were pressed into the service of patriotism and the definition of national identity.

The National Trust embodied both these notions of national heritage and a certain reconciliation between the public interest and private property. The concept of the Trust arose out of the work of the Commons Preservation Society which, since its foundation in 1865, had been conducting legal battles to save common land and stretches of countryside. The Society's inability to acquire land came to be seen as a drawback to its work: it could not, for example, purchase common rights; nor was it able to ensure the future preservation of places it had saved. Members of the Society had hoped that the Government would acknowledge a national duty to preserve places of beauty and historic interest, but the only legislation that had proved acceptable – the Ancient Monuments Protection Act 1882 – provided for state guardianship only of uninhabited monuments, and then only with the willing compliance of the owners.[21] In 1884 the honorary solicitor to the society, Robert Hunter, advocated the creation of a special corporate body to buy and hold land and buildings 'for the benefit of the nation'.[22] It took some time to rally support for the idea, but ten years later the Constitution of the National Trust was drafted and the inaugural meeting resolved that:

> it is desirable to provide means whereby landowners and others may be

> enabled to dedicate to the nation places of historic interest or natural beauty, and for this purpose it is expedient to form a corporate body, capable of holding land, and representative of national institutions and interests.[23]

From the start the Trust had strong links with large landowners so as to be in touch with potential donors or vendors of desirable properties. It sought to work closely with the existing system of private landownership, always eschewing compulsion. As landlordism fell into economic crisis in the 1920s through the combined effects of death duties and depressed agricultural prices, the Trust came to see the greatest threat to the landscape and historic buildings of the countryside as arising from the collapse of the great estates. As the Trust began to campaign for tax relief for the owners, it increasingly voiced an ethos of paternalistic stewardship which presented the traditional, private owner as the most appropriate custodian of country estates and houses, and Trust ownership as strictly a last resort. Robin Fedden, the Trust's historian, neatly expressed this ethos:

> Danger most commonly follows the break-up of estates. Where great landlords are secure, there is less threat to the landscape pattern. From end to end of England, wherever you meet seemly villages and a countryside that speaks of understanding and affection, the chances are that you will be on a large estate. Where such estates exist, and as long as they can survive, the Trust has a limited contribution to make. The landscape is in good hands, and it would be both unnecessary and presumptuous for the Trust to advocate change.[24]

The Trust quickly established its authority as a holding body. In 1907 it was reconstituted as a statutory body by Act of Parliament. The Act gave the Trust the powers to declare its land and buildings inalienable and to create by-laws for their regulation and protection. The unique status of inalienability enjoyed by most of the Trust's properties means that it cannot divest itself of them, nor can they be compulsorily acquired without recourse to Parliament. The original intention was to prevent the Trust from disposing of land it ceased to value and to inspire confidence in donors and supporters that its properties would be preserved in perpetuity. Inalienability has undoubtedly been an important factor in attracting land and finance. The Trust is now the largest private landowner in England and Wales (there is a separate National Trust for Scotland). It owns over 1 per cent of the land surface (including much of the most beautiful and spectacular scenery), as well as over 200 historic buildings and about a quarter of the undeveloped coastline.[25]

The Trust could not have attained this position without the support and encouragement of successive governments. Seen to be fulfilling an important public function, the Trust is regarded, in effect, as a public agency and it enjoys various powers and privileges as a result. As legislation has been passed to preserve buildings and landscape, government has tended to use the existing machinery of the Trust rather than extend its own establishment. In other European countries official agencies perform functions equivalent to those of the National Trust. In Britain, in contrast, the achievement of official policy in the areas of scenic protection, historic preservation, nature conservation, and countryside recreation has come to depend critically on an independent organization, reflecting – in the words of the Trust's historian – a 'possibly well-grounded prejudice against anything that resembles a Ministry of Fine Art'.[26] Arguably, this ambivalent organization embodies a historic and peculiarly British compromise that has harnessed voluntary support and goodwill to a public purpose (currently the Trust's membership stands at over 1.3 million), while minimizing the direct role of the state and fundamentally respecting (even vindicating) property relations. While the Trust is unique, other preservationist institutions combine these same elements in different ways, including such post-war quangos as the Countryside Commission, the Nature Conservancy Council, and English Heritage. Although these are all official agencies, they are statutory bodies responsible to a governing council and are intended to operate with a marked degree of independence from central government; they work closely with the established voluntary organizations (English Heritage even has its own 'membership' scheme); and they seek to co-operate with private owners.

The rural preservation movement in the inter-war years

The Victorian groups were oriented towards protecting specific sites, but by the 1920s the pressures on the countryside were more ubiquitous. It became evident that a much more concerted effort would be needed to introduce broad legal safeguards equal to the threats posed to rural amenities. With the formation of the Council for the Preservation of Rural England (CPRE) in 1926, rural preservation emerged as a significant force in British politics. Though it quickly established county branches, it was predominantly a metropolitan-centred movement comprising a small but influential group of intellectuals, members of the artistic and literary establishments, and the landed aristocracy. They were able to tap the strong strain in English culture, deeply antipathetic to industrialism and all its creations, particularly the modern city. As Patrick Abercrombie, the pioneer town planner, argued, 'the greatest historical monument that we possess, the most essential thing which *is* England, is the Countryside, the Market Town, the Village, the Hedgerow Trees, the Lanes, the Copses, the Streams and the Farmsteads'. These words appeared in the clarion pamphlet, *The Preservation of Rural England*, which he published in 1926, and which led to the establishment of the CPRE.

The CPRE set about lobbying vigorously for controls over urban sprawl and ribbon development, and for the creation of green belts and national parks. Its leaders saw themselves fighting against an avalanche of bricks, concrete, and asphalt. The motor car, new trunk roads, and commuter railway lines were allowing residential development to break loose from the city boundaries. Suburbs mushroomed as cheap mortgages and depressed land prices enabled many white-collar workers to buy a villa or a bungalow, with a garden and a garage for their new Austin 7 or Ford 8. Between 1900 and 1939, the built-up area of London quadrupled.

The Central (now Country) Landowners' Association was one of the constituent organizations of the CPRE, which had strong links with the traditional landowning class, seeing in them a natural ally in combating urbanization. The need to protect agriculture and create conditions in which it could flourish was now part of the conventional wisdom of rural preservation. The preservationists tended to have a highly romantic and idealized view of farming, summed up by G. M. Trevelyan in his *English Social History* in the following terms: 'Agriculture is not merely one industry among many, but is a way of life, unique and irreplaceable in its human and spiritual values.' In a chronic state of depression, farming practices of the time seemed to pose no threat to other rural interests and pursuits.[27] On the contrary, it was felt that the debilitated condition of farming exacerbated many other threats to the countryside, such as urban encroachment, the decline of rural communities, and the flight from the land. Not only was the countryside under attack from the towns, but rural life was disintegrating from within. Farming, secure and revitalized was seen as the essential conserver of both the social life and the natural beauty of the countryside.[28]

Support for protecting the countryside came from two other groups: open-air enthusiasts and naturalists. Hiking, previously a bohemian pursuit, became a popular pastime in the 1920s and 1930s, attracting young people equally from working-class and middle-class backgrounds. The bicycle, the motor car, and the charabanc made the countryside more accessible, while reductions in the working week and declining religious observance gave people more free time and the opportunity for at least temporary escape from drab, smoky, and overcrowded towns. The popularity of hiking derived from the vogue for health and physical fitness and from the new sense of social permissiveness which had emerged in the wake of the First World War. By the early 1930s it was also attracting many of those who were being subjected to the enforced idleness of mass unemployment. Estimates put the number of regular country walkers at over 500,000, with about 10,000 in the Derbyshire Peak district alone during a summer weekend.[29]

A number of organizations were formed to represent and cater for this burgeoning interest. The Ramblers' Association, established in 1935, brought together 600 local rambling clubs with 50,000 members, strongly concentrated in London and the south-east and the industrial areas of the midlands, Yorkshire, Lancashire, and central Scotland. 'Hiking has replaced beer as the shortest cut out of Manchester', quipped Cyril Joad, an influential figure with the Ramblers' Association, in his book *The Untutored Townsman's Invasion of the Country* (1946, p. 17). For the accommodation of this new army of townsfolk seeking the country, the Youth Hostels Association was set up in 1931, with Trevelyan as its President. By the summer of 1939 it had 30 hostels and 83,000 members. These and older organizations, such as the Camping Clubs, the Holiday Fellowship, the Co-operative Holidays Association and the Cyclists' Touring Club, gave their backing to the protection of the countryside, especially the campaign for national parks.

For the Ramblers' Association, however, the main political cause was access to open country. This was an issue which divided the rural preservation movement. The National Trust had become committed to the position that preservation must be its first task and must take precedence over public access and recreation. The CPRE and the Commons Preservation Society wanted extensions of access over private land to be negotiated with landowners. But such a relaxed and constitutional approach (as well as the Trust's élitism) seemed a luxury to hard-pressed walking enthusiasts in many of the northern industrial towns, hemmed in by moorland which, though easily visible from their centres (when the smoke cleared), was often unreachable because of a concerted refusal by landowners to allow access.[30] The lack of rights of way, particularly over the grouse moors of the southern Pennines, was a major source of resentment, and occasioned various mass trespasses and protest demonstrations. The most famous, on Kinder Scout in April 1932, was organized by the British Workers' Sports Federation, an offshoot of the Young Communist League. Several hundred trespassers clashed with gamekeepers and the police, and prison sentences totalling seventeen months were meted out to five of the leaders. Though the official rambling clubs had boycotted it, they and their members were aroused by the severity of the punishment, and this fuelled a broad political campaign and popular crusade to amend the law of trespass.[31]

The other source of support for rural preservation was from naturalists interested in wildlife protection. The largest and most active group was the Royal Society for the Protection of Birds. In the 1930s its membership stood at about 4,000. It had been formed in 1889, initially as a crusade against the fashion for exotic feathers in women's hats which threatened the survival of many of the colourful birds of the Tropics. However, it had broadened its interests to encompass all aspects of wild bird protection, and had played a key role in promoting protective legislation. The main threats to bird propulations were seen to come from the excesses of hunting, gamekeeping, egg collecting, and human cruelty. By the 1920s, though, other hazards to birdlife had begun to exercise the RSPB, including oil pollution and the use of arsenical sprays by fruit growers.[32]

A threat to wildlife of a different kind was recognized by the Society for the Promotion of Nature Reserves, which had been set up in 1912. It was concerned at the loss of wild and natural areas and their attendant species, through such causes as building, land drainage, and woodland clearance. The Society's outlook was influenced by the understanding emerging from the new science of ecology of the causal relationship between habitats and animal and plant communities, which indicated the need to protect habitats to preserve species. It was a relatively inactive group and certainly made no popular impact, but its small membership included leading naturalists and influential public figures.[33]

The countryside in war and the post-war planning system

The cause of rural preservation was greatly advanced by the outbreak of the Second World War. The demand for a 'better Britain', to replace the Britain of the dole queue, means test, and social strife, exerted pressure on the wartime coalition government to demonstrate that it contemplated some decisive changes when the war was over. Planning and the promise of greater prosperity and security, it was realized, could play a major role in stimulating the war effort, so the need to preserve the British countryside was embraced, at least in principle, as part of a general commitment to a comprehensive land use policy. It was a cause which commended itself to the government for its obvious symbolic value in helping sustain morale during a period of intense national sacrifice.

Official preparations for post-war reconstruction provided unprecedented opportunities to influence the formulation of government policy. The major focus for opinions on the future of the countryside was the official Committee on Land Utilisation in Rural Areas, appointed in October 1941 by the Minister of Works and Buildings, Lord Reith, to consider 'the conditions which should govern building . . . in country areas consistent with the maintenance of agriculture . . . having regard to . . . the wellbeing of rural communities and the preservation of rural amenities.'[34] The Committee's Chairman was Lord Justice Scott, who had been Vice-President of the CPRE.

Formulated at the height of the war, the Scott Report's thinking contributed crucially to the post-war ideology of urban containment and green belts, the establishment of national parks and nature reserves, and state support for farming. Its essential thesis was that the rural community was an agricultural community, dependent on the continuance and revival of the traditional mixed character of British farming. The assumption was that a prosperous farming industry would preserve both the rural landscape and rural communities. 'Farmers and foresters are unconsciously the nation's landscape gardeners', declared the report, adding emphatically, 'there is no antagonism between use and beauty' (paras 14, 16c). The major threat to rural areas, apart from government neglect, was seen to arise from building and industrial pressures which, it was argued, threatened to mar the countryside, take land out of farming, and entice labour away from agriculture. The Report was optimistic that, if these pressures could be resisted, if farm incomes were improved, and if modern services were provided in villages, then rural life would be resuscitated and the countryside preserved.

These assumptions had far-reaching consequences, particularly in shaping the philosophy and objectives of post-war policy for agriculture and land-use planning. Thus the Town and Country Planning Act, 1947 accorded farming and forestry a pre-emptive claim over all other uses of rural land. There were two underlying motives: to regenerate agriculture and to protect the countryside from urban development. Britain, more than any other country, had relied on imported food. The war, however, clearly demonstrated the strategic importance of increased home supplies of food and timber as well as the role government could play in stimulating production, and this became the basis of post-war agricultural policy as set out in the Agriculture Act of 1947. This Act and the Town and Country Planning Act of the same year were complementary, in that the former achieved a secure environment for investment in farming and the latter ensured security of land use for agriculture.

The Planning Act introduced the principle that new development and changes in land use were to be subject to control, to ensure their conformity to plans to be prepared by the local planning authorities. In rural areas these were the county councils. The definition of 'development' in the Act specifically excluded 'the use of any land for the purposes of agriculture or forestry (including afforestation), and the use for any of those purposes of any building occupied together with the land so used'. The Act also made possible the undertaking of agricultural operations without planning permission, through the provisions of the general development order. Agriculture's exemption occasioned no dispute at the time – reflecting the romantic view of farming encapsulated in the Scott Report and the overriding political commitment given to the expansion of home food production in a period when rationing was still in force.

The new planning system sought to protect agriculture, not only as an end in itself, but also as a means of achieving the wider aims of rural preservation. The latter objective was elaborated in the National Parks and Access to the Countryside Act 1949. This provided the machinery for the designation and administration of national parks, to be chosen for their landscape and recreational value; areas of outstanding natural beauty (AONBs), chosen on landscape grounds alone; and national nature reserves and sites of special scientific interest (SSSIs) to safeguard places with a special flora, fauna, or geology.[35]

The crude statistics suggest that both the Agriculture Act, 1947 and the Town and Country Planning Act, 1947 have gone some way towards achieving at least their primary objectives. Prior to the war, British agriculture supplied approximately a third of the food requirement for a population of 47 million. Today this has risen to about two-thirds of the food requirements for a population of 56 million, and in terms of temperate foodstuffs Britain is rapidly approaching and exceeding self-sufficiency. The achievements of the planning system in curbing urban sprawl can be seen in the statistics of the loss of farmland to urban development. In the 1930s the average annual rate was over 25,000 hectares. Since the war, this has been cut back to an average annual rate of fewer than 16,000 hectares.[36] In achieving these primary objectives, however, profound changes have occurred to both agriculture and the rural preservation movement – changes which have set these two interests increasingly at odds with one another.

The threat from within

The post-war period has brought considerable social change to rural areas and, in the process, perceptions of the countryside have altered. Rural depopulation continued as in earlier decades, with the number of full-time agricultural workers declining by 400,000 (70 per cent) between 1950 and 1980; and it is still falling at over 10,000 per annum. The new prosperity which state support brought to agriculture did not ensure a place in the sun for farm labourers: their wages have lagged consistently behind the average for industrial workers.[37] Moreover, the whole thrust of technological development in agriculture has been to replace labour with machinery. This has favoured the farmer with capital to draw on, and most of them have expanded their holdings, squeezing out the small farmer.

The loss of population as small farmers and farm workers, or their sons and daughters, sought a better living in urban areas, has been more than matched by the movement of the middle class into the countryside. Growing affluence and car-ownership have enabled more and more people to realize their dream of a home in the country. Tight planning controls around the major cities and the construction of motorways have pushed housing pressures further and further out into free-standing towns and villages.

Thus the great exodus from the cities of retired people, commuters, and second homers has quickly taken up the slack in the housing market created by rural depopulation. This has involved the transfer of much of the existing housing stock from the private, rented sector catering for the rural working class to the owner-occupied sector catering for the ex-urban middle class. Once the housing surplus had been taken up, the pressured rural areas began to experience growing demand for new private housing, but those who have settled in the countryside have sought to use the preservation procedures of the planning system to safeguard their own residential amenity. Thus, most of the expansion which has been permitted for villages and small towns has consisted of small, low-density estates, mainly of bungalows, semi-detached, and detached houses. Many of the prettier villages have been designated as conservation areas; in these, housing development has usually been limited to sensitive in-filling of vacant sites. Such policies simultaneously enhance the attractiveness of the area and restrain new development. The consequent shortage, high quality, and hence high cost, of housing tend to restrict residential access mainly to higher income groups. Moverover, most rural councils have shown a marked reluctance to build low-cost housing for rent, thus further restricting the housing opportunities for those with low incomes.

The ex-urban newcomers show none of the political quiescence of the rural working class. Invariably, they have challenged the political and social leadership of farmers and landowners. Gradually they have taken over many of the established institutions, such as the parish council, the Women's Institute, and the local Conservative Association. They have also established new institutions which reflect their interests and particular visions of the rural community. Indeed, many of the rural issues which have arisen in recent years derive from the expectations which the middle classes have taken with them into the countryside – such as the expectations of urban standards of service provision as well as an unchanging countryside.[38]

One of the most pervasive political expressions of the middle class in the countryside is local amenity and conservation groups. Once settled in their chosen town or village, they are understandably reluctant to see changes that might adversely affect the environmental standards which first attracted them. Most towns and villages now have an amenity or preservation group, formed in the period between 1955 and 1975 and concerned with protecting the character and physical appearance of the locality from any unpleasant developments. They are particular thick on the ground in the south-east, the most prosperous region in Britain, and the area which has experienced the greatest pressures for development; and in retirement areas, such as the west, the Isle of Wight, Cumbria, North Yorkshire, and East Anglia. In comparison, there are few in remote rural areas, which have not yet experienced the full impact of retirement or commuter pressures. All in all, there are about 1,200 local amenity societies in Britain with a combined membership of about 300,000.

The other prominent local groups concerned with environmental protection are the county trusts for nature conservation. Most of these were set up in the late 1950s and early 1960s. There are now 46 trusts covering the country and their total membership stands at 150,000. As well as helping to identify and protect local habitats of importance to wildlife, the trusts acquire sites of their own which they run as nature reserves. Many who join these local groups have swollen the support for groups such as the RSPB, the National Trust, and the CPRE, thus greatly increasing their influence and standing.[39]

By virtue of their own predominantly middle-class membership, many local environmental groups are able to draw on an impressive array of professional expertise, organizational skills, and political contacts, and this often gives them considerable influence, especially within local government. Across most of the countryside they are a significant political force, treated with wary respect by officials and developers. They are particularly effective at working within the planning system, making use of the opportunities provided for public participation and the various protective designations in order to stave off unwanted urban development.

To the latter-day rural preservationists, however, there is a worm in the bud threatening their vision of an unchanging countryside, and that is modern agriculture. Few people anticipated the rapid transformation in agricultural practices which was to occur in the post-war period. Even so, agricultural intensification, fostered by government and realized through the adoption of new technologies, the spread of mechanization, and the consolidation of holdings, has transformed the rural environment. As the scale of the post-war revolution in agriculture has become apparent, there has been a shift in emphasis in preservationist circles from a focus on urban and industrial pressures as the main threat to landscape and wildlife to a preoccupation with the destructive effects of changing farming and forestry practices and technologies. This shift has involved profound changes in the popular image of agriculture. The sheer pace of development has destroyed any illusions that it is intrinsically an unchanging or slowly evolving activity. Nowadays, many conservationists regard agriculture as austere and capitalistic, no longer the embodiment of rural simplicity and rustic virtue. In the title of a recent, highly publicized book by Marion Shoard, a former staff member of the CPRE, farmers are accused of *The Theft of the Countryside* (1980).

Yet disillusionment on the part of those concerned about the protection of the countryside has come about in a slow and piecemeal fashion, so strong was the romantic view of farming. To the inter-war preservationists, the countryside was an abstract symbol. What actually happened in the real countryside mattered less than that it should be defended from the incursions of urban industrialism. As the middle classes have moved into rural areas, so the realities of the countryside have gradually impinged on their Arcadian vision.

Since the late 1950s, through a series of controversies, the image of the farmer as the conserver of the countryside has gradually disintegrated, to be replaced by the image of the agri-businessman. It was the introduction of factory production methods, particularly the building of broiler houses from the mid-1950s onwards, that first aroused alarm, drawing attention to the anomaly whereby industrial-type buildings – often badly sited and of poor design – could be erected without any form of consultation if intended for agricultural use. Pressure from amenity societies, planners, and the County Councils' Association secured an amendment to the general development order in 1960 which brought agricultural buildings of more than 5,000 sq. ft. in area within the remit of development control. A further modification in 1967, in this case in response to the threat of tower silos, brought agricultural buildings over 40 ft. in height under development control.

The deaths of thousands of birds in 1960 and 1961 after the spring sowing of seeds dressed with Aldrin and Dieldrin prompted concern over the threat that a chemicalized agriculture posed to wildlife. The resultant public outcry prompted the chemical manufacturers to establish a voluntary system restricting the availability of the more toxic pesticides.[40] In an effort to avert criticism, the manufacturers suggested that other factors might be contributing to the decline in bird numbers, and even funded research into the effects of hedgerow removal. The loss of hedgerows reached its peak in the 1960s at 10,000 miles per annum and is still perhaps the most unpopular consequence of mechanization in agriculture. Investigations by naturalists, however, suggested that this was of marginal importance to wildlife populations in the lowlands compared to the diminishing area of deciduous woodland, so attention was again switched to another facet of modern agricultural practice.

Agricultural intensification has pressed more and more upon marginal land, as new technology and grants from the Ministry of Agriculture have encouraged the improvement of land which previously was relatively unproductive. In the early 1960s, public attention was first directed to the ploughing-up of moorland in Exmoor. The Exmoor Society, a branch of the CPRE, commissioned a study of the extent of change and this suggested that the very fabric of the national park was under threat. Ever since, the Exmoor issue has been at the forefront of debate on the future of the countryside, though concern has also been aroused since the mid-1970s at the conversion of moorland in other national park and upland areas. In the late 1960s the reclamation of old pasture and the ploughing-up of lowland heaths and downland were also brought into focus; and in the 1970s the drainage of wetland habitats received some of the most concentrated publicity.[41]

Thus, over a period of about twenty years the various environmental implications of agricultural intensification have been recognized, one by one, first by conservationists and then by others, including an increasing number of farmers. Because each issue was viewed separately, the response of the conservation organizations was to seek specific remedies through isolated campaigns. It is only within the last decade that a global concept of agricultural change seems to have been fully grasped. The Countryside Commission's *New Agricultural Landscapes* study of 1974 was influential in demonstrating that changes in agriculture could comprehensively alter 'the landscape' rather than just individual features of it, though the Commission was optimistic that, with proper guidance, modern agriculture could produce a new, though equally attractive, countryside, largely through planting or conserving the areas that farmers had no use for. Since then opinions have hardened, as evidence of a general destruction of habitats has accumulated.[42]

The sweeping impact of agricultural development on the rural environment has drawn attention to the failure of existing protective measures to moderate or deflect the tide of change. National parks and AONBs cover 19 per cent of England and Wales; and SSSIs 5 per cent. Farming and forestry occupy 90 per cent of the land so designated, but local planning authorities lack any control over these uses. This means that the measures intended to safeguard the countryside are impotent in relation to the forces now recognized as dominant in the creation or destruction of landscape and habitats. Moreover, the Ministry of Agriculture and the Forestry Commission continue to give grants in designated areas to encourage agricultural intensification and afforestation.

With the growing appreciation of the totality of agricultural change, the whole system of agricultural support has come under attack as the root cause of intensification, rather than the activities of individual famers. The system of protective designation has also been questioned, not only because of its ineffectiveness, but also for neglecting the ordinary countryside and its depredations by dividing the country into areas where conservation mattered and areas where it could be ignored with impunity. Pressure has thus built up for general powers to regulate the environmental impact of agricultural and forestry development. In seeking these and other changes, the conservation lobby now confronts a powerful set of interests which it once regarded as its closest allies.

Notes

1 Thomas, 1983, 28.
2 ibid., 301.
3 Armytage, 1961; Hardy, 1979; Kumar, 1978.
4 Burrow, 1966.
5 Wiener, 1981.
6 Marsh, 1982, 36–7.
7 Keith, 1975.
8 Marsh, 1982, 36–7.
9 Hewison, 1987; Newby, 1987; Wiener, 1981; Williams, 1973; Wright, 1985.

10 But see Webber, 1986, ch. 4.
11 John Betjeman in Fawcett, 1976, 56–73.
12 Fleming, 1961, 219–36; Houghton, 1957.
13 Rothschild, 1914, 416–18.
14 Horwood, 1913, 629–37.
15 Egerton, 1973, 322–50.
16 Meldola, 1883, 447–9.
17 Meldola, 1880.
18 Lankester, 1915; Mitchell, 1912, 478–87.
19 Kennet, 1972.
20 M. Hunter, in Lowenthal and Binney, 1981, 22–32.
21 Kennet, 1972.
22 Hunter, 1884; Murphy, 1987.
23 Murphy, 1987, 108.
24 Fedden, 1974.
25 Lowe and Goyder, 1983, ch. 8.
26 Fedden, 1974.
27 Trevelyan, 1944, 554; Collins, 1985, 38–46.
28 Sheail, 1981.
29 J. Lowerson, in Gloversmith, 1980, 258–80.
30 C. Hall, in Gill, 1976, 162–75.
31 Hill, 1980.
32 Sheail, 1976.
33 P. D. Lowe, in Warren and Goldsmith, 1983, 329–52; Lowe, 1976, 517–35.
34 *Report of the Committee on Land Utilisation in Rural Areas*, Cmnd 6378, London, HMSO, 1942.
35 Cherry, 1975; Sheail, 1976.
36 Best, 1981.
37 Newby, 1977.
38 Newby, 1980.
39 Lowe and Goyder, 1983, ch. 8.
40 Sheail, 1985.
41 Lowe, Cox, MacEwen, O'Riordan, and Winter, 1986.
42 *Nature Conservation and Agriculture*, London, Nature Conservancy Council, 1977.

Bibliography

Acland, Lady Anne, 1976, *Holnicote Estate, Somerset*, London, National Trust.

Allen, William, 1846, *Life of William Allen, With Selections from His Correspondence*, London, Charles Gilpin.

Andrews, William, 1888–9, *North Country Poets*, Basingstoke, Marshall, Morgan & Scott.

Armytage, W. H. G., 1961, *Heavens Below*, London, Routledge & Kegan Paul.

Arnold, M. (ed.), 1879, *The Poems of Wordsworth*, London, Macmillan.

Arnold, Matthew, 'The Scholar Gipsy', 'Thyrsis', in Kenneth Allott (ed.), 1965, *The Poems of Matthew Arnold*, London, Longman.

Ashford, L. J., 1960, *The History of the Borough of High Wycombe from its Origins to 1880*, High Wycombe Public Library.

Barry, Alfred, 1867, *The Life and Works of Sir Charles Barry*, London, John Murray.

Best, R. H., 1981, *Land Use and Living Space*, London, Methuen.

Best, R. H. and Anderson, M. A., 1984, 'Land use structure and change in Britain, 1971 to 1981', *The Planner*, November.

Bielckus, C. L., Rogers, A. W., and Wibberley, G. P., 1972, *Second Homes in England and Wales*, Wye, Kent, Wye College.

Blomfield, Reginald and Thomas, F. Inigo, 1892, *The Formal Garden*, London, Macmillan.

Bloomfield, R., 1803, *The Farmer's Boy*, 7th edn, London, Verner & Hood.

Booker, J., 1974, *Essex and the Industrial Revolution*, Chelmsford, Essex County Council.

Borrow, George [1851], 1907, *Lavengro*, London, John Murray.

—— [1857], 1907, *The Romany Rye*, London, John Murray.

Boyson, Rhodes, 1970, *The Ashworth Cotton Enterprise: The Rise and Fall of a Family Firm, 1818–1880*, Oxford, Clarendon Press.

BPP (British Parliamentary Papers) 1888 LIV, LV, LVII, London, RC Market Rights and Tolls, Asst Commissioners' Reports.

Brewster, D. M. M., 1970, 'Tadcaster in 1851: the population of a market town', *Annual Report and Bulletin of the West Riding (Northern Section) Committee of the National Register of Archives*, Wakefield, National Register of Archives.

Brightfield, M. F., 1968, *Victorian England in its Novels, 1840–1870*, Los Angeles, University of California Library.

Brontë, Emily [1847], 1965, *Wuthering Heights*, Harmondsworth, Penguin.

Burrow, J. W., 1966, *Evolution and Society*, Cambridge, Cambridge University Press.

Burton, T. L., 1967, *Windsor Great Park: A Recreation Study*, Wye, Kent, Wye College.

Burton, T. L. and Wibberley, G. P., 1965, *Outdoor Recreation in the British Countryside*, Wye, Kent, Wye College.

Cavendish, Lady Frederick, 1927, *Diary*, John Bailey, (ed.), London, Batsford.

Chalklin, C. W. (ed.), 1975, *Early Victorian Tonbridge*, Maidstone, Kent County Library.

Champion, A. G., 1981, *Counterurbanisation and Rural Rejuvenation in Rural Britain. An Evaluation of Population Trends since 1971*, Seminar Paper no. 38, Department of Geography, University of Newcastle upon Tyne.

Charlton, Barbara, 1949, *Recollections of a Northumbrian Lady 1815–1866*, L. E. O. Charlton, (ed.), London, Jonathan Cape.

Cherry, G. E., 1974, *The Evolution of British Town Planning*, London, Leonard Hill.

—— 1975, *Environmental Planning 1939–1969*, vol. II, *National Parks and Recreation in the Countryside*, London, HMSO.

Cholmondeley, Mary [1897], 1968, *Red Pottage*, London, Anthony Blond.

Clapham, J. H., 1926–51, *An Economic History of Modern Britain*, 3 vols, Cambridge, Cambridge University Press.

Clare, John, 1827, *The Shepherd's Calendar*, London, James Duncan.

Clark, Roger, 1975, *Somerset Anthology*, York, William Sessions.

Clifford, Derek, 1962, *A History of Garden Design*, London, Faber.

Cobbett, William [1830], 1967, *Rural Rides*, Harmondsworth, Penguin.

Coleman, Alice, 1976, 'Is planning really necessary?', *Geographical Journal*, CXLII, 3.

Collins, E. J. T., 1985, 'Agriculture and conservation in England: an historical overview 1880–1939', *Journal of the Royal Agricultural Society of England*, CXLVI.

Cook, E. T. and Wedderburn, Alexander (eds), 1903–12, *The Complete Works of John Ruskin*, London, George Allen.

Cooper, A., 1971, 'Victorian Newark', *Transactions of the Thoroton Society*, LXXV.

Cooper, Nicholas, 1967, 'Housing the Victorian poor', *Country Life*, 8 June, 1454–7.

Cooper, T. Sidney, RA, 1890, *My Life*, London, Richard Bentley & Son.

Coppock, J. T., 1962, 'The changing arable in England and Wales', in R. H. Best and J. T. Coppock, *The Changing Use of Land in Britain*, London, Faber.

—— 1977, *Second Homes: Curse or Blessing?*, Oxford, Pergamon.

Coppock, J. T. and Prince, H. C., 1964, *Greater London*, London, Faber.

Countryside Commission, 1974, *Farm Recreation and Tourism in England and Wales*, The Commission.

Cullingworth, J. B., 1975, *Reconstruction and Land Use Planning 1939–47*, London, HMSO.

—— 1985, *Town and Country Planning in England and Wales*, 9th edn, London, Allen & Unwin.

Dana, R. H., 1921, *Hospitable England in the 1870's*, London, John Murray.

Darley, Gillian, 1975, *Villages of Vision*, London, Architectural Press.

Dickens, Charles [1836–7], 1972, *The Pickwick Papers*, Harmondsworth, Penguin.

—— [1840], 1972, *The Old Curiosity Shop*, Harmondsworth, Penguin.

—— [1849–50], 1966, *David Copperfield*, Harmondsworth, Penguin.
Disraeli, Benjamin, 1938, *Letters to Frances Anne, Marchioness of Londonderry, 1836–61*, Marchioness of Londonderry, (ed.), London, Macmillan.
—— [1845], 1954, *Sybil or: The Two Nations*, Harmondsworth, Penguin.
Dower, M., 1965, *The Fourth Wave: The Challenge of Leisure*, London, Civic Trust.
Duckworth, A. M., 1971, *The Improvement of the Estate: A Study of Jane Austen's Novels*, Baltimore, Johns Hopkins University Press.
Eastlake, C. L. [1872], 1970, *A History of the Gothic Revival*, J. M. Crook, (ed.), Leicester, Leicester University Press.
Egerton, F. N., 1973, 'Changing concepts of the balance of nature', *Quarterly Review of Biology*, XLVIII.
Eliot, George [1859], 1951, *Adam Bede*, London, Dent.
—— [1866], 1966, *Felix Holt*, London, Dent.
—— 1876, *Daniel Deronda*, London, Blackwood.
Elliott, D. J., 1975, *Buckingham: The Loyal and Ancient Borough*, Chichester, Phillimore.
Elliott, E., 1829, *The Village Patriarch*, n.p.
Emerson, P. H., 1887, *Pictures from Life in Field and Fen*, London, G. Bell.
Everitt, A. M. (ed.), 1973, *Perspectives in Urban History*, London, Macmillan.
Fawcett, J. (ed.), 1976, *The Future of the Past*, London, Thames & Hudson.
Fedden, R., 1968, *The Continuing Purpose*, London, Longman.
—— 1974, *The National Trust: Past and Present*, London, Cape.
Fleming, D., 1961, 'Charles Darwin, the anaesthetic man', *Victorian Studies*, IV.
Forbes, Christopher, 1975, *The Royal Academy (1837–1901) Revisited*, Princeton, NJ, Art Museum, Princeton University.
Fothergill, S. and Gudgin, G., 1982, *Unequal Growth: Urban and Regional Employment Change in the UK*, London, Heinemann Educational.
Fowler, J., 1894, *Recollections of Old Country Life*, London, Longman.
Franklin, Jill, 1973, 'The planning of the Victorian country house', unpublished thesis, University of London.
—— 1975, 'Troops of servants: labour and planning in the country house 1840–1914', *Victorian Studies*, XIX, 2.
Freeman, M. D., 1976, 'A history of corn milling, *c.* 1750–1914, with special reference to south central and south eastern England', unpublished Ph.D. thesis, University of Reading.
Frye, Northrop, 1957, *Anatomy of Criticism*, Princeton, NJ, Princeton University Press.
Fullerton, Lady Georgiana, 1847, *Grantley Manor*, London, n.p.
Gardner, Robert, 1852, *History, Gazetteer and Directory of the County of Oxford*, Peterborough, Robert Gardner.
Gaskell, Elizabeth [1855], 1925, *North and South*, London, John Murray.
—— 1857, *The Life of Charlotte Brontë*, London, Smith Elder.
Gill, C. (ed.), 1976, *The Countryman's Britain*, Newton Abbot, David & Charles.
Gillispie, G. C., 1951, *Genesis and Geology: A Study in the Relations of Scientific Thought, Natural Theology and Social Opinion in Great Britain, 1790–1950*, Cambridge, Mass., Harvard University Press.
Gilpin, William, 1782, *Observations on the River Wye*, London, n.p.
—— 1786, *Observations . . . Made in the Year 1772*, London, n.p.
—— 1798, *Observations on the Western Parts of England*, London, n.p.
Girouard, Mark, 1971, *The Victorian Country House*, Oxford, Clarendon Press.

Gittings, Robert, 1975, *Young Thomas Hardy*, London, Heinemann.
Gloversmith, F. (ed.), 1980, *Class, Culture and Social Change: A New View of the 1930s*, Hassocks, Sussex, Harvester Press.
Gore, Mrs, 1849, *The Diamond and the Pearl*, London, Colburn.
Great Victorian Pictures, 1978, London, Arts Council of Great Britain.
Green, B. H., 1985, *Countryside Conservation*, 2nd edn, London, Allen & Unwin.
Greening, A., 1971, 'Nineteenth century country carriers in north Wiltshire', *Wiltshire Archaeological and Natural History Magazine*, LXVI.
Hadfield, Alice M., 1970, *The Chartist Land Company*, Newton Abbot, David & Charles.
Hadfield, Miles, 1960, *Gardening in Britain*, London, Hutchinson.
Haggard, H. Rider, 1902, *Rural England*, London, Longman.
Hall, P., 1988, 'The Industrial Revolution in reverse', *The Planner*, January.
Hall, P., Thomas, R., Gracey, H., and Drewett, R., 1973, *The Containment of Urban England*, London, Allen & Unwin.
Hanscomb, C. E., 1967, *Common Blood*, London , Queen Anne Press.
Hardie, Martin, 1968, *Water-Colour Painting in Britain: III The Victorian Period*, London, Batsford.
Hardy, D., 1979, *Alternative Communities in Nineteenth Century England*, London, Hartman.
Hardy, Thomas, [1872], 1974, *Under the Greenwood Tree*, London, Macmillan.
—— [1874], 1974, *Far from the Madding Crowd*, London, Macmillan.
—— [1878], 1974, *The Return of the Native*, London, Macmillan.
—— [1880], 1974, *The Trumpet-Major*, London, Macmillan.
—— [1886], 1974, *The Mayor of Casterbridge*, London, Macmillan.
—— [1887], 1974, *The Woodlanders*, London, Macmillan.
—— [1891], 1974, *Tess of the d'Urbervilles*, London, Macmillan.
—— [1896], 1974, *Jude the Obscure*, London, Macmillan.
Havinden, M. A., 1966, *Estate Villages, A Study of the Berkshire Villages of Ardington and Lockinge*, London, Lund Humphreys
Henkin, L. J., 1963, *Darwinism in the English Novel, 1860–1950*, New York, Russell & Russell.
Hewison, R., 1987, *The Heritage Industry*, London, Methuen.
Hill, H., 1980, *Freedom to Roam*, Ashbourne, Derby., Moorland Publishing, Derbys.
Hirsch, F., 1977, *Social Limits to Growth*, London, Routledge & Kegan Paul.
Holderness, B. A., 1972, ' "Open" and "Close" parishes in England in the eighteenth and nineteenth centuries', *Agricultural History Review*, XX, 2.
Holroyd, Abraham, 1871, *Saltaire and its Founder, Sir T. Salt, Bart.*, Yorks, Saltaire.
Horn, Pamela, 1976, *Labouring Life in the Victorian Countryside*, Dublin, Gill & Macmillan.
Horne, Eric, 1930, *What the Butler Winked At*, London, T. W. Laurie.
Horwood, A. R., 1913, 'The State protection of wild plants', *Science Progress*, VII.
Houghton, W., 1957, *The Victorian Frame of Mind*, New Haven, Mass., Yale University Press.
Howitt, William [1838], 1844, *The Rural Life of England,* London, Longman.
Hunt, W. H., 1886, 'The Pre-Raphaelite Brotherhood: a fight for art', *Contemporary Review*, XLIX.

Hunter, R., 1884, *A Suggestion for the Better Preservation of Open Spaces*, Commons Preservation Society.

Hussey, Christopher, 1958, *English Country Houses: Late Georgian*, London, Country Life.

Jefferies, Richard [1878], 1948, *The Gamekeeper at Home*, London, Oxford University Press.

—— [1879], 1948, *The Amateur Poacher*, London, Oxford University Press.

—— [1879], 1949, *Wild Life in a Southern County*, London, Lutterworth.

—— [1880], 1949, *Hodge and His Masters*, London, Eyre & Spottiswoode.

—— [1880], 1948, *Round About a Great Estate*, London, Eyre & Spottiswoode.

—— [1884], 1947, *The Life of the Fields*, London, Lutterworth.

—— [1885], 1948, *The Open Air*, London, Eyre & Spottiswoode.

—— [1889], 1948, *Field and Hedgerow*, London, Lutterworth.

Jekyll, Gertrude, 1899, *Wood and Garden*, London, Longman.

Jekyll, Gertrude and Weaver, Lawrence, 1912, *Gardens for Small Country Houses*, London, Country Life.

Jenkins, G., 1972, *The Craft Industries*, London, Longman.

Joad, C. E. M., 1946, *The Untutored Townsman's Invasion of the Country*, London, Faber & Faber.

Jones, Bernard (ed.), 1962, *William Barnes, The Poems*, Carbondale, Ill., Southern Illinois University Press.

Keeble, D. and Gould, A., 1985, 'Entrepreneurship and manufacturing firm formation in rural regions: the East Anglian case', in M. J. Healey and B. W. Ilberry, *The Industrialisation of the Countryside*, Norwich, Geo Books.

Keith, W. J., 1975, *The Rural Tradition*, Hassocks, Sussex, Harvester Press.

Kelly, 1898, *Kelly's Directory of Bedfordshire, Huntingdonshire and Northamptonshire*, East Grinstead, Kelly's Directories.

Kennet, W., 1972, *Preservation*, London, Temple Smith.

Kerr, Robert, 1864, *The Gentleman's House, Or How to Plan English Residences from the Parsonage to the Palace*, London, John Murray.

Kingsley, Charles [1850], 1881, *Yeast: A Problem*, London, Macmillan.

Knightley, Lady Julia, 1915, *Journals 1856–1884*, Julia Cartwright (ed.), London, John Murray.

Knoepflmacher, U. C. and Tennyson, G. B. (eds), 1977, *Nature and the Victorian Imagination*, Berkeley, Calif., University of California Press.

Kumar, K., 1978, *Prophecy and Progress*, Harmondsworth, Penguin.

Lanceley, William, 1925, *From Hall-boy to House Steward*, London, Edward Arnold.

Lankester, R., 1915, *Diversions of a Naturalist*, London, Methuen.

Lawton, R., 1973, 'Rural depopulation in nineteenth-century England', in D. R. Mills (ed.), *English Rural Communities: The Impact of a Specialised Economy*, London, Macmillan.

Lee, J. M., 1956, 'The rise and fall of a market town: Castle Donington in the nineteenth century', *Leicestershire Archaeological and Historical Society Transactions*, XXXII.

Lethaby, W. R., 1935, *Philip Webb and his Work*, Oxford, Oxford University Press.

Lewis, S., 1840, *Topographical Dictionary of England, III*, London, S. Lewis & Co.

Little, Bryan, 1974, *Portrait of Somerset*, London, Robert Hale.

Loudon, J. C., 1833, *An Encyclopaedia of Cottage, Farm and Villa Architecture*, London, Longman.

—— [1840], 1970, *The Landscape Gardening and Landscape Architecture of the Late Humphrey Repton*, London, Gregg International.
Lowe, P. D., 1976, 'Amateurs and professionals: the institutional emergence of British plant ecology', *Journal of the Society for the Bibliography of Natural History*, VII.
Lowe, P. D. and Goyder, J. M., 1983, *Environmental Groups in Politics*, London, Allen & Unwin.
Lowe, P. D., Bradley, T., and Wright, S., 1986, *Deprivation and Welfare in Rural Areas*, Norwich, Geo Books.
Lowe, P. D., Cox, G., MacEwen, M., O'Riordan, T., and Winter, M., 1986, *Countryside Conflicts: The Politics of Farming, Forestry and Conservation*, Aldershot, Hants, Gower.
Lowenthal, D. and Binney, M. (eds.), 1981, *Our Past Before Us: Why Do We Save It?*, London, Temple Smith.
Lusk, Lewis, 1901, *The Life and Work of Benjamin Williams Leader, R.A.*, Coulsdon, Surrey, Art Annual, Virtue & Co.
McEwen, A. and McEwen, M., 1987, *Greenprints for the Countryside: The Story of Britain's National Parks*, London, Allen & Unwin.
McLaughlin, B., 1986a, 'Rural policy in the 1980s: the revival of the rural idyll', *Journal of Rural Studies*, II, 1.
—— 1986b, 'The rhetoric and reality of rural deprivation', *Journal of Rural Studies*, II.
Marks, John George, 1896, *Life and Letters of Frederick Walker, A.R.A.*, London, Macmillan.
Marsh, J., 1982, *Back to the Land: The Pastoral Impulse in Victorian England from 1880 to 1914*, London, Quartet.
Meldola, R., 1880, *An Inaugural Address Delivered to the Epping Forest and County of Essex Naturalists' Field Club, 28 February 1880*, Essex Naturalists' Field Club, Buckhurst Hill, Essex.
—— 1883, 'The conservation of Epping Forest from the naturalists' standpoint', *Nature*, XXVII.
Mill, J. S., 1873, *Autobiography*, London, Longman.
Ministry of Works and Planning, 1942, *Report of the Committee on Land Utilisation in Rural Areas*, London, HMSO.
Mitchell, P. C., 1912, 'Zoological gardens and the preservation of fauna', Annual Report of the British Association.
Moss, G. (ed.), 1976, *Britain's Wasting Acres*, London, Architectural Press.
Murphy, G., 1987, *The Founders of the National Trust*, Beckenham, Croom Helm.
Murphy, S. F. (ed.), 1883, *Our Homes and How to Make them Healthy*, Eastbourne, Cassell.
Muthesius, H., 1904–5, *Das Englische Haus*, Berlin, Wasmuth.
Nash, Charles, 1845, *The Goodrich Court Guide*, 2nd edn, London, Hereford.
Neale, K., 1974, *Victorian Horsham: The Diary of Henry Michell 1809–1874*, Chichester, Phillimore.
Newby, H., 1977, *The Deferential Worker*, London, Allen Lane.
——, 1979, *Green and Pleasant Land? Social Change in Rural England*, London, Hutchinson.
—— 1987, *Country Life*, London, Weidenfeld & Nicholson.
Pahl, R. E., 1965, *Urbs in Rure: The Metropolitan Fringe in Hertfordshire*, Geography Paper No. 2, London School of Economics and Political Science.
—— 1966, 'The social objectives of village planning', *Official Architecture and*

Planning, XXIX, 8, reprinted as ch. 2 of R. E. Pahl, 1970, *Whose City? and Further Essays on Urban Society*, London, Longman.
Parris, Leslie, 1973, *Landscape in Britain c. 1750–1850*, London, Tate Gallery.
Patmore, J. A., 1983, *Recreation and Resources*, Oxford, Blackwell.
Perry, P. J., 1974, *British Farming in the Great Depression 1870–1914: An Historical Geography*, Newton Abbot, David & Charles.
Pevsner, Nikolaus, 1952, *The Buildings of England: North Devon*, Harmondsworth, Penguin.
—— 1953, *The Buildings of England: Derbyshire*, Harmondsworth, Penguin.
—— 1957, *The Buildings of England: Northumberland*, Harmondsworth, Penguin.
—— 1958, *The Buildings of England: North Somerset and Bristol*, Harmondsworth, Penguin.
—— 1961, *The Buildings of England: North Lancashire*, Harmondsworth, Penguin.
—— 1964, *The Buildings of England: Lincolnshire*, Harmondsworth, Penguin.
Pevsner, Nikolaus, *et al.*, 1951–74, *The Buildings of England*, Harmondsworth, Penguin.
Price, Sir Uvedale, 1794–8, *An Essay on the Picturesque as Compared with the Sublime and the Beautiful: And on the Use of Studying Pictures for the Purpose of Improving Real Landscape*, Hereford, n.p.
Ricks, C. (ed.), 1969, *Tennyson: Poems*, London, Longman.
Robinson, William, 1883, *The English Flower Garden*, London, John Murray.
Rodee, Howard D., 1977, 'The "Dreary Landscape" as a background for scenes of rural poverty in Victorian paintings', *Art Journal*, XXXVI, 4 (College Art Associaton of America).
Rogers, A., 1972, *This was their World: Approaches to Local History*, London, British Broadcasting Corporation.
Rogers, A. W., 1985, 'Local claims on rural housing: a review', *Town Planning Review*, LVI, 3.
Rogers, A. W., Blunden, J., and Curry, N., 1985, *The Countryside Handbook*, Beckenham, Croom Helm.
Rosenblum, Robert, 1961, 'The abstract sublime', in Henry Geldzahler, *New York Painting and Sculpture: 1940–1970*, London, Pall Mall Press.
Rothschild, N. C., 1914, 'The preservation of nature', *Countryside*, n.d.
Saint, Andrew, 1976, *Richard Norman Shaw*, New Haven, Conn., Yale University Press.
Saville, J., 1957, *Rural Depopulation in England and Wales 1851–1951*, London, Routledge & Kegan Paul.
Scharf, Aaron, 1974, *Art and Photography*, Harmondsworth, Penguin.
Scott, G. G., 1857, *Remarks on Domestic and Secular Architecture*, London, John Murray.
Sheail, J., 1976, *Nature in Trust: the History of Nature Conservation in Britain*, Glasgow, Blackie.
—— 1981, *Rural Conservation in Interwar Britain*, Oxford, Clarendon Press.
—— 1985, *Pesticides and Nature Conservation: The British Experience 1950–1975*, Oxford, Clarendon Press.
Shoard, Marion, 1980, *The Theft of the Countryside*, London, Temple Smith.
Smigelski, R., 1978, *Self-supporting Cooperative Village*, Building & Social Housing Foundation.
Smith, D. H., 1933, *The Industries of Greater London*, London, King.
Smith, S., 1971, 'Alfred Waterhouse', unpublished thesis, University of London.

Staley, Allen, 1973, *The Pre-Raphaelite Landscape*, Oxford, Clarendon Press.
Stanton, Phoebe, 1971, *Pugin*, London, Thames & Hudson.
Stevenson, J. J., 1880, *House Architecture*, London, Macmillan.
Story, Alfred T., 1892, *The Life of John Linnell*, London, Richard Bentley & Son.
Surtees, Robert Smith [1843], 1926, *Handley Cross, or Mr Jorrocks's Hunt*, Bath, Baynton.
—— [1846], 1904, *The Analysis of the Hunting Field*, London, Methuen.
—— [1853], 1958, *Mr Sponge's Sporting Tour*, London, Oxford University Press.
—— [1865], 1921, *Mr Facey Romford's Hounds*, London, Methuen.
Tennyson, Alfred, *In Memoriam, Maud*, in Christopher Ricks (ed.), *The Poems of Tennyson*, London, Longman.
Theuriet, André, 1892, *Jules Bastien-Lepage and his Art: A Memoir*, London, T. Fisher Unwin.
Thomas, A., 1978, *The Expanding Eye*, Beckenham, Croom Helm.
Thomas, K., 1983, *Man and the Natural World: Changing Attitudes in England 1550–1800*, London, Allen Lane.
Thompson, F. M. L., 1963, *English Landed Society in the Nineteenth Century*, London, Routledge & Kegan Paul.
Tibble, J. W. (ed.), 1935, *John Clare: Poems*, London, Dent.
Ticknor, George, 1864, *Life of William Hickling Prescott*, London, Routledge, Warne & Routledge.
Trevelyan, G. M., 1944, *English Social History*, London, Longmans, Green & Co.
Trollope, Anthony [1858], 1957, *Doctor Thorne*, London, Dent.
—— 1869, *Phineas Finn, the Irish Member*, London, n.p.
Victoria County History: Bedfordshire II, 1908, W. Page (ed.), London, Archibald Constable.
Victoria County History: Oxfordshire II, 1907, W. Page (ed.), London, Archibald Constable.
Victoria County History: Oxfordshire X, 1972, Alan Crossley, (ed.), London, Oxford University Press.
Victoria County History: Yorkshire East Riding II, 1974, K. J. Allison, London, Oxford University Press.
Vining, D. R. and Kontuly, T., 1978, 'Population dispersal from major metropolitan regions: an international comparison', *International Regional Science Review*, III, 1.
Warren, A. and Goldsmith, F. B. (eds), 1983, *Conservation in Perspective*, Chichester, Wiley.
Webber, G. C., 1986, *The Ideology of the British Right 1918–1939*, Beckenham, Croom Helm.
Whetham, E. H., 1952, *British Farming 1939–49*, Walton-on-Thames, Nelson.
Wiener, M. J., 1981, *English Culture and the Decline of the Industrial Spirit 1850–1980*, Cambridge, Cambridge University Press.
Wilde, Oscar [1895], *The Importance of Being Earnest*, in *Oscar Wilde: Selected Writings*, 1961, London, Oxford University Press.
Williams, Merryn, 1972, *Thomas Hardy and Rural England*, London, Macmillan.
Williams, R., 1973, *The Country and the City*, London, Chatto & Windus.
Wilson, Charles, 1954, *The History of Unilever, A Study in Economic Growth and Social Change, I*, Eastbourne, Cassell.
Woodbridge, K, 1971, *The Stourhead Landscape*, London, National Trust.

Wordsworth, William, *The Excursion*, in *Poetical Works of Wordsworth*, 1960, London, Oxford University Press.
Wright, P., 1985, *On Living in an Old Country: The National Past in Contemporary Britain*, London, Verso.
Yonge, Charlotte, 1853, *The Heir of Redclyffe*, London, Macmillan.

Index